Experimentation for Marketing Decisions

KEITH K. COX   BEN M. ENIS
University of Houston

INTERNATIONAL TEXTBOOK COMPANY
Scranton, Pennsylvania

International's Series in Marketing Research

Consulting Editor

Ralph L. Day

*Professor of Business Administration
Graduate School of Business
Indiana University*

Standard Book Number 7002 2225 1

Copyright ©, 1969, by International Textbook Company

All rights reserved. No part of the material protected by this copyright notice may be reproduced or utilized in any form or by any means, electronic or mechanical, including photocopying, recording, or by any informational storage and retrieval system, without written permission from the copyright owner. Printed in the United States of America by The Haddon Craftsmen, Inc., Scranton, Pennsylvania. Library of Congress Catalog Card Number: 74-76404.

Preface

In our experience with courses in marketing research, we have felt that, in general, the area of experimentation has not received the attention it deserves. Experimentation has much to offer marketing management in facilitating decision making, and in advancing marketing knowledge. It is an area which is expanding rapidly in terms of theoretical knowledge and in application to marketing problems. Consequently, we have prepared this volume primarily to supplement standard material in marketing research courses at the undergraduate and graduate levels. The book will also be of interest to marketing practitioners who desire a nontechnical overview of experimentation in marketing. A third area in which the book can be useful is in courses in statistical methods.

Our objective has been to prepare an introduction to the subject of experimentation in marketing research and decision making. Our purpose was to provide for the reader a means of understanding the concepts, techniques and potential applications of experimentation, for managerial use and/or as a prelude to the study of standard works in the field. Consequently, the text assumes that the reader has had some exposure to the field of marketing, either through coursework or experience, and has some basic knowledge of statistical inference and probability.

Many people contribute to the preparation of any textbook. From the work of scholars and practitioners in the field of experimentation, we have drawn inspiration, insight, and example. Our colleagues, Ralph L. Day (consulting editor of this series), Charles L. Broome, James E. Willis, and James B. Higginbotham read the manuscript and offered numerous helpful comments. Mrs. Gwen Florence, Mrs. Rebecca Davis, and other members of the staff of the Center for Research in Business of the

University of Houston provided invaluable secretarial assistance. Of course, we alone bear responsibility for the finished work.

KEITH K. COX
BEN M. ENIS

Houston, Texas
February 1969

Contents

part I   **CONCEPTS OF EXPERIMENTATION ... 1**

     1. Introduction to Experimental Research 3
     2. The Experimental Method. 15
     Selected Bibliography 24

part II   **TECHNIQUES OF EXPERIMENTAL DESIGN ... 27**

     3. Completely Randomized Designs 29
     4. Randomized Blocks Designs 39
     5. Latin Square Designs 48
     6. Factorial Designs. 62
     Selected Bibliography. 73

part III   **APPLICATION OF EXPERIMENTATION TO MARKETING DECISION MAKING ... 75**

     7. Experiments in Distribution, Pricing, and Product Policies 77
     8. Experiments in Promotion 90
     9. Managerial Aspects of Experimentation 101
     Selected Bibliography 111

     Appendix A   Table of Random Numbers 115

     Appendix B   The F Distribution 116

     Index 121

part *I*

CONCEPTS OF EXPERIMENTATION

This part introduces the basic concepts of experimentation. The purpose of the section is to provide a theoretical foundation for Part II: Techniques of Experimental Design, and Part III: The Application of Experimentation to Marketing Decision Making. To secure this foundation, the reader should obtain from Part I a familiarity with the terminology of experimentation, a "feel" for the nature of experimentation and its relationship to scientific research in general, and a basic understanding of the objectives, constraints, and analytical techniques of experimental design. The theme of this part is that experimentation is a scientific procedure which can be as valuable to the marketing discipline as it has been to the physical sciences, medicine, and agriculture.

chapter *1*

Introduction to Experimental Research

Marketing is the process of matching consumers' needs and the firm's resources. The conditions that affect this dynamic matching procedure are complex. Marketing managers must analyze these conditions in order to make decisions that are profitable to the firm. For this reason, increasing emphasis is being placed on the use of those concepts and methods of marketing research which lend themselves to and facilitate the process of rational analysis for decision making. The area of experimentation comprises one such group of marketing research techniques.

PURPOSE OF THIS BOOK

This book will acquaint the marketing student with the fundamentals of experimental research. The basic experimental designs which appear to be useful for marketing decision making are examined. However, comprehensive coverage of the complete area of experimental design is not attempted. A thorough study of this book will equip the reader to understand and analyze experimentation in marketing. The reader should also develop the ability to plan and carry out simple experiments, but he probably will not develop technical expertise in experimental design. The purpose of this book, then, is to contribute to managerial competence in marketing, by extending the marketing student's knowledge in one important area of research: experimental design and execution.

USES OF EXPERIMENTATION IN MARKETING

To illustrate our statement that experimentation is useful for marketing decision making, here are some representative questions to which marketing management might want answers.

1. Can we increase profits by servicing small accounts by mail rather than from branch stores?
   Answer: Yes, says Charles H. Sevin on the basis of an experiment reported in Chapter 7, pp. 77-79.
2. Can we increase supermarket sales of our product by obtaining additional shelf space?
   Answer: We can for certain types of products, according to the Cox experiment reported in Chapter 7, pp. 79-82.
3. Will the addition of stannous fluoride to our toothpaste reduce users' cavities?
   Answer: Yes, according to the Muhler experiments (Chapter 7, pp. 86-87).
4. Does the number of times that a salesman calls on a particular account in a given time period affect the size of the order obtained from that account?
   Answer: No. (See the Cox experiment in Chapter 8, pp. 92-93).
5. Is a given newspaper advertisement more effective in color than in black-and-white?
   Answer: Yes, according to the Long Beach *Press-Telegram* experiment (Chapter 8, pp. 93-94).
6. Which of several promotional techniques is most effective in selling winter pears?
   Answer: Store demonstrations and dealer contests are both superior to media advertising and special point-of-purchase displays, according to the U. S. Department of Agriculture (Chapter 8, pp. 94-96).
7. Is it necessary for an advertisement to change the subject's attitude in order to cause him to use more of the product?
   Answer: No, says Valentine Appel (Chapter 8, pp. 98-99).

These answers represent only a small sample of potential uses of experimentation in marketing. These and other experiments are reported in Chapters 7 and 8, so the interested reader might turn immediately to these chapters and broaden his knowledge of actual applications of experimentation in marketing. However, these reports are presented in summary form. The detailed explanations of the forms and the underlying methodology of each form are presented in the first six chapters of this text.

OBJECTIVE OF EXPERIMENTAL RESEARCH

The study of any subject should begin with a statement of its objectives. The objective of experimental research is to measure the effect of

Introduction to Experimental Research

alternative courses of action (termed treatments) upon a certain dependent variable (e.g., sales volume, consumers' attitudes), while controlling the effects of extraneous variables. The usefulness of experimental designs in marketing extends across the functional areas of promotion, distribution, pricing, and product policies. Wherever marketing management is interested in measuring the effects of alternative courses of action, experimentation may be a practical means of reducing the risk involved in deciding among the alternatives. As Banks has stated,

> The goal of experimental design is the confidence that it gives the researcher that his experimental treatment is the cause of the effect he measures.[1]

Experimentation differs from alternative methods of marketing research in that in experimentation the researcher manipulates the independent variable or variables before measuring the effect upon the dependent variable. For example, the effect of price changes on the sales volume of a particular product can be examined by actually varying the price of the product. A nonexperimental approach would be to ask consumers whether they would buy more of the product if more were displayed. The manipulation of independent variables, together with procedures for controlling extraneous variation—i.e., the effects of variables other than the variable being manipulated—forms the basis of the power of experimental research relative to other research techniques. The better the researcher's control over the experiment variable and extraneous variation, the more confident the researcher can be that he is in fact determining cause and effect relationships.

FOUNDATIONS OF EXPERIMENTAL DESIGN

Experiments are designed to test explanations of observed events. In their classic work, Cohen and Nagel differentiate the scientific method of gaining knowledge from three other methods of knowing (tenacity, authority, and intuition) since only the scientific method permits doubt and encourages modification of knowledge as new evidence is accumulated.[2] Scientific inquiry attempts to understand the cause(s) of natural events by proposing certain explanations, and then testing the relationship of the explanation to the actual event. The explanation is then tentatively accepted or modified according to the test results.

---

[1] Seymour Banks, "Designing Marketing Research to Increase Validity," *Journal of Marketing* (October 1964), pp. 32–40.
[2] M. R. Cohen and Ernest Nagel, *An Introduction to Logic and Scientific Method* (New York: Harcourt, Brace & World, Inc., 1934), pp. 191-196.

This procedure of continuous inquiry, tentative explanation, testing, reassessment, and further inquiry inevitably leads to increasing understanding of and knowledge about the phenomena being studied. Experimentation is the most conclusive of scientific testing procedures. Indeed, many researchers are reluctant to accept as valid any cause-and-effect explanation which has not been verified by experimentation. Thus experimentation is the hallmark of scientific research.

Experimental design in the physical sciences (e.g., physics, chemistry) consists of procedures through which the researcher controls, i.e., hold relatively constant, all variables except those whose effects he intends to measure. In the biological and social sciences, it is usually not possible for the researcher to follow such procedures. In agriculture, for example, the researcher cannot control differences in soil composition and amount of rainfall. In marketing, he cannot control differences in such factors as individual tastes, exposure to outside stimuli, and competitors' actions. Despite these difficulties, advances have been made in experimental research in the biological and social sciences which in some respects parallel developments in the physical sciences.[3] Since most of this work originated outside the field of marketing, some of it is unfamiliar to most marketing students.

Experimental designs are based upon the concept of inductive logic. Certain facts are assembled and analyzed. Conclusions drawn from these facts are then used to *induce* generalizations about the overall situation from which the facts are taken. Specifically, a sample is drawn from the universe and used to estimate the universe value. Suppose, for example, that a researcher wanted to determine the average food expenditures of a population of six families. He could take a census, i.e., ask each of the six families for its expenditure. He would then sum these figures and divide by six to obtain the mean expenditure. Alternatively, the researcher could draw a sample from the population and use the sample results to estimate the population average. This procedure might be useful if, for example, the families were geographically separated.

If the researcher decided to draw a sample of three families from the population, there are 20 possible distinct combinations of families of which our sample can be comprised.[4] He would ask each sample family

---

[3] The classic text in the field of experimental design is Ronald A. Fisher, *The Design of Experiments,* 7th ed. (Edinburgh, Scotland: Oliver and Boyd, Ltd., 1960).

[4] The reader will remember that the number of sample combinations of size r which can be drawn from a population of size n is given by

$$\frac{n!}{r!(n-r)!}$$

for its expenditure, sum these and divide by three to obtain the sample mean. He can then use this statistic to estimate the population mean. The researcher has *induced* the general situation from an analysis of a few facts. Provided that the sample is a valid estimate of the universe value, the concept of inductive logic is useful to marketing management because it generally provides a faster and less costly means of measuring the universe value than would result from a measurement of all elements of the universe.

Sample validity, then, is an important consideration. There are two aspects of validity: internal validity and external validity.[5] Internal validity is concerned with the usefulness of the experiment itself. The question to be answered is—was the experimental treatment responsible for the results obtained? In general, internal validity is subject to statistical control. That is, the amount of error in measurements of treatment effects can be determined for specific levels of confidence.

The essence of statistical control is that within every source of extraneous variation to be statistically controlled, a randomizing process is carried out so that the extraneous variation has equal exposure among the treatment variables. Consider the problem of controlling variation in sales between test stores over the life of an experiment. Such differences can distort the results of the experiment. Since it is physically impossible to keep the sales of each test store physically constant over time, the differences may be statistically controlled through a randomizing process. Randomization is accomplished by allowing chance to govern the assignment of treatments to test units. As most marketing experiments are designed to compare alternative treatments in order to select the best alternative, only a relative measure is needed for comparison, not an absolute answer. By randomizing extraneous variation so that each possible treatment is given equal exposure, the absolute answers may change but the relative answers should fluctuate only as a result of random error, which can be measured in formal experimental designs through replicating the experiment.

The following example illustrates the concept of statistical control. We wish to determine the effectiveness of a particular package design relative to a certain other package design. If the two packages (treatments) are essentially equal in effect on sales, then the mean sales rates of the different packages will differ only as a result of the effects of extraneous

---

[5]This discussion follows Donald T. Campbell and Julian C. Stanley, "Experimental and Quasi-Experimental Designs for Research on Teaching," in N. L. Gage, ed., *Handbook of Research on Teaching* (Chicago: Rand McNally & Co., 1963), pp. 171-246.

forces and random sampling error. To insure the internal validity of this experiment, we will want to control the effect of such extraneous variables as the price of the product, differences in test stores, and differences between time periods.[6] In symbols, the problem can be stated as follows:

$$\text{Sales of } A = A + X + Y + Z$$

and

$$\text{Sales of } B = B + X + Y + Z$$

where A = sales effect of treatment A
B = sales effect of treatment B
X = sales effect of price
Y = sales effect between test stores
Z = sales effect between time periods

The difference in effectiveness is then given by

$$\text{Sales of } A - \text{sales of } B = (A - B) + (X - X) + (Y - Y) + (Z - Z)$$
$$= A - B$$

Since we are interested in the relative difference in sales effectiveness between A and B, the effects of X, Y, and Z are neutralized as long as they affect A and B equally. In the actual test, however, we are likely to obtain the following sample results:

$$\text{Sales of } A = A + X + y_1 + z_1$$

$$\text{Sales of } B = B + X + y_2 + z_2$$

where y_1 and y_2 are sample estimates of Y, and z_1 and z_2 are sample estimates of Z. (The sales price, X, need not be estimated, since it is a known parameter.)

Consequently, the difference in sales effectiveness is

$$\text{Sales of } A - \text{sales of } B = (A - B) + 0 + (y_1 - y_2) + (z_1 - z_2)$$

Differences between stores and time periods cannot be physically eliminated, but can be statistically controlled by randomly allocating the test treatments to stores and time periods, and by replicating the entire experiment. These procedures increase the internal validity of the experiment.

External validity, on the other hand, pertains to generalization of the results obtained. The relevant question is —Do the results of this experiment apply to other situations? Since generalization involves consideration of factors beyond the data generated in the experiment, external validity is

---

[6]The reader will recognize that numerous potential sources of additional extraneous variation exist. Our hypothetical example is limited to three such sources to simplify the explanation of the concept.

not subject to statistical control. Careful planning and implementation of the experiment can increase external validity, but the amount of the increase cannot be determined. Nevertheless, attention must be given to the question of external validity. There is little point in performing an internally perfect experiment if the results obtained tell us nothing about the realities of the market place.

Experimentation may be performed "in the field" or under laboratory conditions. The packaging experiment mentioned above could actually be performed in the store (field), or in an artificial laboratory environment specifically arranged for the purpose. In general, field experimentation presents more difficulties with regard to internal validity than do laboratory experiments, but is more useful for purposes of external validation. That is, conditions in the field are most difficult to control because they are more realistic. Useful research has been performed both in the field and in the laboratory.

OPERATIONAL DECISION RULES

Research is "useful" to marketing management if and only if it provides some operational method of reducing the uncertainty associated with decision making. Such procedures generally take the form of explicit criteria or "decision rules." The conventional method of evaluating information obtained from sampling is termed "hypothesis testing." A hypothesis in this sense is a postulated statement or assumption about a given population. The researcher attempts to accept or reject the hypothesis, on the basis of statistical information about the population obtained from a probability sample.

Statistical data can in many cases be expressed in terms of mean values. In such cases the hypothesis can be operationally tested by assuming that the hypothesis has no significance, i.e., that the sample means do not differ except as a result of chance fluctuations. This assumption is the null hypothesis (H_0), which can be accepted or rejected by comparing the sample mean with predetermined standards or with other sample means. The alternate hypothesis is that the means do differ significantly.

Under this procedure, the decision maker has two choices: accept or reject H_0. Whether or not the choice made is the correct one depends upon the actual condition of the population. If the null hypothesis is true and is accepted by the decision maker, then the decision is correct. The correct decision is also made when a false hypothesis is rejected. If the decision maker rejects a true H_0, or accepts a false H_0, he has made an error.

These errors are referred to as type I and type II errors respectively. Table 1-1 summarizes the decision choices and their consequences.

TABLE 1-1
Summary of Hypothesis-Testing Consequences

Decision	Actual Population Condition	
	H_0 is True	H_0 is False
Accept H_0	Correct decision	Type II error (β)
Reject H_0	Type I error (α)	Correct decision

The usual approach to hypothesis testing is to specify in advance a probability level for the error of rejecting a true H_0 (type I error). This probability is referred to as the alpha (α) risk, and is the percentage of incorrect rejections of the true H_0 which would be expected to occur simply because of random variation in a very large number of independent samples. The null hypothesis is rejected if the actual probability that H_0 is true is less than the predetermined alpha risk level. Naturally, the smaller the alpha risk selected, the smaller is the probability of committing a type I error. Unfortunately, for a given sample size, as the alpha risk is reduced, the probability of accepting H_0 when it is in fact false increases. This probability is referred to as a type II error or as the beta (β) risk. This risk is measured by $1 - \beta$, the "power of the significance test." The larger the beta risk, the less power has the alpha-risk test of significance. In actual practice, the beta risk is often determined after the sample has been taken, or is ignored. This procedure for establishing the validity of a certain hypothesis can therefore be summarized in the following four steps:

1. Formulate a null hypothesis of the form: The sample means do not differ significantly.
2. Select a significance level (traditionally, the .05 and/or .01 levels are selected).
3. Perform the appropriate statistical test of the data (F test, t test, Z test, chi-square test).
4. Compare the statistical result to the predetermined significance level, and accept or reject the hypothesis on the basis of this comparison.

For decision-making purposes in marketing, too much emphasis has at times been placed upon the level of significance (controlling a type I error), and too little emphasis placed upon the power of the test (controlling

Introduction to Experimental Research

a type II error).[7] Let's take a typical marketing situation to illustrate this point.

Suppose that the marketing manager is introducing a new product in a regional market. From past experience he concludes that there are three possible promotional strategies which might be used in the initial promotional campaign. These are (1) couponing through the mail, (2) door-to-door distribution of free samples of the new product, and (3) demonstrations in retail outlets. If each of these promotional choices costs about the same amount of money, a decision could be made using the hypothesis-testing approach as follows. First, an experiment would be conducted. The null hypothesis would be that all three promotional strategies are equally effective. The alternative hypothesis would state that all three promotional tools are not equally effective. Some level of significance is then selected (usually the 5 percent or 1 percent level). The appropriate statistical test is applied, and the null hypothesis is accepted or rejected on the basis of the sample results.

Under this approach, the type I error is controlled, but the type II error has been largely ignored. Yet in many decision situations in marketing the loss resulting from a type I error is negligible, while a type II error could prove very costly. In the case of making a type I error in the choice of the best promotional strategy for a new-product introduction, suppose that we rejected the true hypothesis (concluded that one promotional strategy was better than the others) even though all were in fact equally effective. Since we have to select one of the equally effective alternatives, there is actually little risk associated with our choice of strategies.

On the other hand, we might accept the hypothesis (conclude that there is no difference in the effectiveness of the three promotional strategies) when one promotional strategy is in fact more effective than the others. This type II error could be very expensive, in terms of opportunity costs, if we select one of the less effective strategies. For a given sample design with a particular sample size, decreasing the probability of a type I error will increase the probability of a type II error. For this reason there is a sound managerial basis for using a 10 or 25 percent level of significance rather than the traditional 1 or 5 percent level in many marketing decision situations. This point is illustrated in more detail in the examples presented in Part II.

---

[7] For an excellent discussion of this point, see Samuel B. Richmond, *Statistical Analysis,* 2d ed. (New York: The Ronald Press Company, 1964), Chapter 10, especially pp. 248-250.

DEFINITION OF TERMS

The purpose of this book is to explain experimentation. In order to facilitate communication with the reader, we discuss at this point some basic terminology.

The term *test unit* denotes the subject of the experiment, i.e., the entity which responds to the experiment. In marketing, the test units are generally people (consumers), stores, or sales territories. The response of the test unit, e.g., change in consumers' attitudes or level of store sales, is the dependent variable of the experiment.

The term *treatment* is used to denote the different test variables introduced to the test unit by the researcher.

The term *extraneous variables* is used to denote all other variables which affect the response of the test unit. Various procedures, discussed below, are employed to eliminate or control these variables.

The term *observation* denotes the actual result of a given treatment effect upon a particular test unit.

Treatment effects in informal experimentation are analyzed by comparing the value of the dependent variable after treatment application to the before-treatment value of that variable, and/or to the value of the comparable dependent variable which did not receive the treatment application. The measurement of the treatment effects in formal experimental designs is performed by means of techniques collectively termed *analysis of variance*. The following terms are associated with analysis of variance.

The sample variance s^2 is given by

$$s^2 = \frac{\sum_{i=1}^{n}(y_i - \bar{y})^2}{n-1}$$

where y_i = individual values $(i = 1, \ldots, n)$
n = number of values

$$\bar{y} = \text{mean value} = \frac{1}{n}\sum_{i=1}^{n} y_i$$

This statistic is an unbiased estimate of the population variance.

Introduction to Experimental Research

The numerator of the variance is termed the *sum of squares*, and is obtained by subtracting the mean from the values, squaring the differences, and summing.

The denominator of the variance is termed *degrees of freedom*. The degrees of freedom are determined by the number of independent linear comparisons which can be made among the n observations. Specifically,

$$\text{Degrees of freedom} = \begin{bmatrix} \text{number of inde-} \\ \text{pendent obser-} \\ \text{vations on} \\ \text{source of} \\ \text{variations} \end{bmatrix} - \begin{bmatrix} \text{number of inde-} \\ \text{pendent param-} \\ \text{eters estimated} \\ \text{in computing} \\ \text{variations} \end{bmatrix}$$

For example, where the population mean is estimated from a random sample of size n, the number of degrees of freedom is one less than the sample size,[8] $(n-1)$.

One of the most important mathematical features of variance analysis is the fact that both the numerator (sum of squares) and the denominator (degrees of freedom) can be subdivided into various subgroups that sum to the total sum of squares and degrees of freedom. The term *mean square* is used to describe the various variance estimates in analysis of variance, and is computed by dividing each of the sums of squares by the appropriate degrees of freedom.

The *residual* or *experimental error* is that part of the total variation which is not accounted for or controlled in the experiment. It is due to the effects of extraneous variables which have not been statistically removed from the data, and to random errors of measurement.

Analysis of variance results are interpreted by using the F *ratio*. The F ratio is a ratio between two variance estimates. If there is no difference between treatment means, then the numerator of the F ratio, i.e., the treatment mean square, should exceed the denominator (residual error mean square) only as a result of sampling error. The larger the F ratio, the greater is the probability that the treatment means are not equal. Critical values of the

---

[8] For additional explanation of degrees of freedom, see Edward D. Bryant, *Statistical Analysis* (New York: McGraw-Hill Book Company, 1960), pp. 48-49; and B. J. Winer, *Statistical Principles in Experimental Design* (New York: McGraw-Hill Book Company, 1962), pp. 51-53.

F ratio for various levels of statistical significance are given in the appendix. The term *replication* means that the testing of a group of treatments in the experimental design is repeated, perhaps several times. Replication is desirable because it increases the precision of estimates of the experimental error.

The term *randomization* means that a chance selection process is used to assign the treatments within the experiment, rather than basing the assignment of treatments upon the researchers' judgment. Randomization is vitally important to experimental design because it provides a basis for ascribing observed significant differences to differences in treatment means rather than to extraneous causes.[9]

ORGANIZATION OF THIS BOOK

This chapter has introduced the topic of experimental research, which can be useful in many marketing decision-making situations. The purpose of experimentation is to measure the effect of certain treatments upon specified dependent variables. Inductive logic provides the conceptual basis for experimentation. Experimental results are evaluated by hypothesis testing. Methodological problems are of two types: internal control and external generalization. Succeeding chapters examine alternative ways of meeting these problems, and present examples of the use of experimental designs in actual marketing situations.

Chapter 2 discusses the experimental method. Emphasis is placed upon describing the experimental method and upon evaluating various types of experimental designs. Part II (Chapters 3-6) presents four basic formal experimental designs for marketing decision making: completely randomized, randomized blocks, Latin square, and factorial designs. In Part III, applications of experimental research techniques to marketing are reviewed. Attention is given to experimental work in the functional areas of distribution, pricing, product policy, and promotion. The contribution of experimental research to marketing decision making is stressed throughout the book and summarized in Chapter 9.

[9]For a more complete discussion of randomization, see Bernard Ostle, *Statistics in Research*, 2d ed. (Ames, Iowa: Iowa State University Press, 1963), p. 249.

chapter 2

The Experimental Method

In the preceding chapter the objectives of experimental research were stated, and the methodological foundations of experimentation were discussed. This chapter examines the design and implementation of experimental research. Several elementary designs are presented and evaluated. To facilitate reader understanding, a specific, hypothetical marketing problem is introduced and is continued through Chapter 6. As more rigorous and precise designs are presented, the reader can relate these designs to the marketing problem faced by the "Jonesco Soap Company." The reader, therefore, has a common basis for understanding each design, and has a means of comparing and analyzing the various designs.

HYPOTHETICAL PROBLEM: THE JONESCO SOAP COMPANY

Our hypothetical illustration concerns the marketing problems of the Jonesco Soap Company. Jonesco is a small, established manufacturer of proprietary soap and related medicinal skin ointments. The company is a family-owned and operated business. Distribution is through drug wholesalers. The company's products are sold nationally, but the bulk of sales are concentrated in the midwest. The company's leading product is "JoBar," a proprietary face and hand soap.

Chemical analysis and tests by dermatologists have confirmed that Jonesco products are of high quality, and are beneficial to their users. The products have been sold for a number of years, and have developed a core of intensely loyal customers. Sales volume, however, has not expanded significantly in the last decade, while marketing and production costs have risen rapidly. Consequently the company is experiencing a profit squeeze which the president, Mr. Jones, believes can be eliminated by increasing sales.

Thus the company faces a common marketing problem: how to convince consumers that a particular product will satisfy their needs, given certain internal and external constraints (e.g., budget limitations, employee skills, competitors' actions) upon marketing decisions. Due to these constraints, and for simplicity, Jonesco's approach to this problem will be limited to alternative packaging considerations. Other marketing strategy variables such as amount of advertising, channel of distribution selection, and pricing changes are not explicitly considered. This problem is used to illustrate the application of experimental techniques in marketing. We begin with ex post facto (nonexperimental) observations, which often lead to simple, rather informal experimental designs, and gradually proceed to more formal designs.

Nonexperimental Observation

The ex post facto or after-the-fact observation is not really planned experimentation. It is merely an observation made after some independent variable has changed. Businessmen make such observations all the time. Here is an example:

> Mr. Jones knows that sales of his products have not increased as rapidly as sales of competing products. He has noticed that several competitors have made changes in their packages. On the basis of this nonexperimental observation, Mr. Jones concludes that the more attractive packaging caused the increased sales of his competitors' products.

In the subjective world of decision making, nonexperimental observations can be valuable to management. These observations take advantage of existing information, and are often based upon logical assumptions (e.g., a more attractive package caused sales to increase). However, such observations can be misleading. One major problem in this example is the implicit assumption that all other variables besides packaging have been held constant or have not influenced the change in sales. However, here are some other possible explanations of higher competitors' sales:

1. Some competitors improved their product quality the previous year, which helped increase their sales.
2. One competitor's field sales force shifted some of its effort to obtain better cooperation with the large supermarket chains, which helped increase sales.
3. Jonesco experienced a long union strike, which limited Jonesco sales.

The Experimental Method

4. The Jonesco Company held prices constant throughout the year, while two competitors slightly decreased their prices.
5. There was an increase in advertising expenditures by some competitors.

Other equally plausible explanations of the sales increases could be listed. Because the nonexperimental observation technique does not control extraneous variation, it has limited value in predicting cause-and-effect relationships. The different causes of sales changes are generally confounded together, so that an accurate measurement of causal relationships may be distorted. Nevertheless, nonexperimental observations may be helpful to decision makers as a first step in formulating assumptions and hypotheses. For example, Mr. Jones might decide to test his hypothesis that more attractive packaging can cause increases in sales. He could change the traditional black paper wrapping on JoBar to a colorful red cardboard container, perhaps with a series of beauty tips printed on the carton. If he made this packaging change, Mr. Jones would be interested in determining the effect of this change upon sales. There are a number of types of informal research designs which Jones could employ.

Informal Experimentation

Informal experimentation can be distinguished from formal experimentation on the basis of error measurement. Informal designs do not provide for the measurement of experimental error, i.e., the random effect of sampling variation, upon the measurements. Despite this limitation, informal designs can be useful to marketing research. These designs are generally less expensive to conduct, in terms of money and time, than are the more formal designs to be considered in Part II. In some business situations, accuracy is less important than speed and/or budget considerations. For this reason, three basic types of informal experimental designs are examined: (1) before-and-after without control, (2) after-only with control, and (3) before-and-after with control.

In all three designs, the test treatment is the substitution of the new, colorful red carton for the traditional black package. This treatment will be introduced into certain sales territories. Other territories will continue to sell the traditional package, and will therefore constitute the control group. The dependent variable, sales volume, will be measured in both sets of territories. Ideally, the territories participating in the experiment are divided equally among the experimental set and the control set. The assumption is that the experimental and control groups are equivalent with respect to those extraneous factors which might influence the experimental results. In this case, such factors as total sales potential, customer buying characteristics, amount of competition, and climatic conditions should be approximately equal for the experimental and control groups.

Before-and-After Without Control Design. In the before-and-after without control experiment, no control group is used. Sales of the traditional package are measured in certain territories, either from existing sales records or by store audit. Denote this value by Y_1. Then the new package is introduced into the territories for the same length of time. Sales of the new package are then measured. Denote this value by Y_2. The treatment effect, or influence of the new package on sales, is measured by subtracting period two sales from period one sales. That is, the treatment effect equals $Y_2 - Y_1$. Figure 2-1 illustrates the before-and-after design. (The arrow indicates passage of the specified time period.)

Test Groups | Sales Before Exposure to Test Treatment (Y_1) → Sales After Exposure to Test Treatment (Y_2)

Treatment effect = $Y_2 - Y_1$

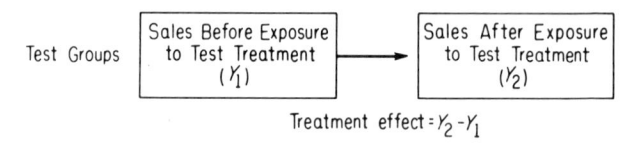

Fig. 2-1. Before-and-after without control design.

Let us assume that sales of the traditional package, Y_1, averaged 10 cases per store during the one-month period. During the second month, sales of the new package, Y_2, averaged 12 cases per store. The treatment effect would then be

$$12 - 10 = 2$$

cases per month. On the basis of this increase in sales, we would tend to believe that the new package has had a positive effect. However, other factors may also have influenced the result.

First, the time periods were not identical. Consequently, specific events may have occurred, and certain key factors, e.g., buyer attitudes, may have changed. Also, the fact that sales were being measured might have caused distributors' salesmen to devote more effort than normal to the product. And, of course, the measurements may have been inaccurate. Researchers refer to these types of changes as history, maturation, testing effect, and instrumentation respectively.[1]

After-Only with Control Design. The after-only with control design

---

[1] See Donald T. Campbell and Julian C. Stanley, "Experimental and Quasi-Experimental Designs for Research on Teaching," in N. L. Gage, ed., *Handbook of Research on Teaching*, (Chicago: Rand McNally & Co., 1963), pp. 171–246, for a more complete discussion of these factors.

improves upon the ex post facto observation by instituting a control group to provide some indication of the effect of extraneous factors. Also, the after-only with control design eliminates possible testing effects inherent in the before-and-after design by not measuring the dependent variable before the treatment is introduced. This design makes the assumption that relevant extraneous factors are equivalent in the experimental and control groups.

In terms of the Jonesco Company problem, the new package could be assigned to certain sales territories for a specified time period. After that period, sales could be measured in the experimental territories, and compared to sales of the traditional package in equivalent territories. The treatment effect is sales volume in the experimental territory, Y_2, minus sales volume in the control territory, X_2. Figure 2-2 illustrates this design.

Experimental Territory → Sales of New Package (Y_2)

Control Territory → Sales of Old Package (X_2)

Treatment effect = $Y_2 - X_2$

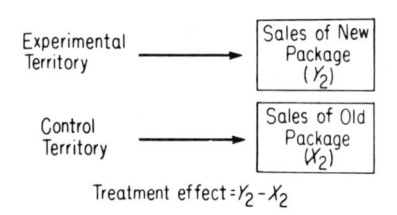

Fig. 2-2. After-only with control design.

The design of Fig. 2-2 suffers from a basic weakness that is difficult to surmount in marketing research. The assumption of equivalence of factors which might affect sales between the experimental and control territories may be expensive and difficult to satisfy. Also, the effects of history, maturation, and instrumentation remain.

Before-and-After with Control Design. The before-and-after with control design combines the advantages of the after-only with control and before-and-after without control designs. The experimental and control territories participate in both before-and-after phases of the experiment, and both are measured before and after the treatment is introduced. Jonesco Company could measure sales in two equivalent territories, introduce the new package into one of them for a specified period of time, then measure sales in the two territories. Figure 2-3 illustrates this design. The treatment effect is $(Y_2 - Y_1) - (X_2 - X_1)$, where Y is experimental group sales, X is control group sales and the subscripts 1 and 2 denote before and after measurements respectively.

Differences in sales in the experimental territory are attributable to both the treatment variable (introduction of the new package) and to the

```
Experimental      Sales Before New         Sales of New
 Territory        Package Introduced  ──▶   Package
                       ($Y_1$)                ($Y_2$)

 Control          Sales Before New         Sales of Old
 Territory        Package Introduced  ──▶   Package
                       ($X_1$)                ($X_2$)
```

Treatment effect = $(Y_2 - Y_1) - (X_2 - X_1)$

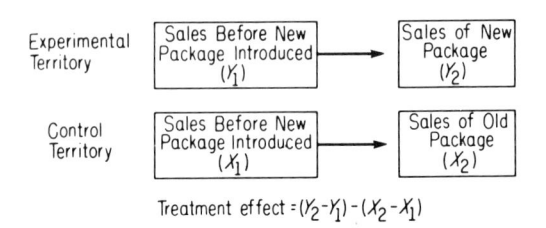

Fig. 2-3. Before-and-after with control design.

effect of extraneous factors. Differences in sales in the control territory are attributable only to the effect of extraneous factors. If the equivalence assumption is made for extraneous variables in the control and experimental territories, then subtracting the control difference from the experimental difference leaves the net effect of the treatment variable. That is, the difference between before-and-after sales in the experimental territory are divided into differences due to extraneous factors and differences due to the influence of the new package. After the adjustment for differences due to extraneous factors, as measured by the control territory, the remaining difference is attributable to the introduction of the new package.

This design is frequently used by researchers in marketing. It is more complex than the other types of informal experimental designs discussed

TABLE 2-1

Characteristics of Informal Designs: Group Participation

Measurement Period	Before and After Without Control		After Only with Control		Before and After with Control	
	Test Group	Control Group	Test Group	Control Group	Test Group	Control Group
Measurement before treatment....	Yes	No	No	No	Yes	Yes
Test treatment.......	Yes	No	Yes	No	Yes	No
Measurement after treatment.....	Yes	No	Yes	Yes	Yes	Yes

here, but less so than the formal designs presented in Part II. All three types of informal designs, as well as more involved types, are used in marketing research primarily because they are less expensive than formal designs, in terms of amount of capital needed, time consumed, and level of researcher skill required. Table 2-1 summarizes the characteristics of the three informal designs discussed in this chapter.

The major limitation of informal designs is the reliance on the equivalence assumption. Informal designs assume that the effect of extraneous variables on the dependent variable is constant over time, and over experimental and control groups. This assumption is open to question in marketing, where many variables affect sales and such other dependent variables as consumer attitudes, preferences, and awareness of advertising. It is quite likely that these effects are not equal, i.e., that there is some degree of experimental error present. Informal designs do not provide any means of measuring this error.

Formal Experimental Designs—An Overview

It was pointed out in Chapter 1 that experimental designs are based on the concept of inductive logic. By taking samples, one can make inferences about universe values. Formal experimental design differs from informal experimentation in that the errors inherent in the sampling process of formal designs can be measured, given certain assumptions which are less restrictive than the equivalence assumption. As noted in Chapter 1, formal experimental designs are evaluated by means of analysis of variance. Ferber and Verdoorn explain analysis of variance as follows:

> Variance analysis is essentially a method for ascertaining from sample data whether one factor really influences another factor or whether the observed association was probably the result of sampling fluctuations. The technique has the advantage of allowing for the influence of such other factors for which data may be available, and in fact permits the simultaneous determination of the significance of each factor in turn on the characteristic under study. It possesses the further advantage of yielding estimates of the relative importance of each of the factors that are found to be significant.[2]

When the experimental data are evaluated using analysis of variance, three assumptions underlie the evaluation. These assumptions are that:

1. The treatment effects and the environmental effects are additive.

[2] Robert Ferber and P. J. Verdoorn, *Research Methods in Economics and Business* (New York: The Macmillan Company, 1962), p. 80.

2. The experimental errors are independently distributed from observation to observation in a normal or Guassian curve.[3]
3. The separate variance estimates are all estimates from a common variance.

In actual experimentation, these statistical assumptions are not always fulfilled. There have been a number of studies which have attempted to analyze the implications of deviations from these assumptions.[4] Fortunately for researchers, the general conclusion of such studies is that the F test (the determinant of statistical significance in analysis of variance) is a robust test. That is, deviations from the mathematical assumptions may not seriously weaken the validity of the experimental results.

Four types of formal experimental designs are presented in Part II. Chapter 3 introduces the completely randomized design, and presents the methodology of analysis of variance. The next three chapters are devoted to refinements of the completely randomized design. The randomized blocks design, Latin square design, and factorial design are presented in Chapters 4, 5, and 6 respectively. These designs allow the application of the analysis of variance technique to the more complex situations within which marketing managers must make decisions.

SIMPLIFICATION OF EXPERIMENTAL EXAMPLES

This book is concerned with the application of experimental research in the general decision-making areas of marketing. In the chapters of Part II, the experimental examples will be simplified in three ways. First, the Jonesco packaging problem continues to serve as a unifying theme and as a basis for comparison among designs. We believe that the reader can attain a better understanding of the techniques if he can relate them to one simplified example which becomes increasingly familiar to him.

Second, only experimental designs with sample treatments of equal size will be discussed and illustrated. This condition is not too difficult to achieve in marketing research. The researcher can usually designate the

---

[3] One means of overcoming this restriction is to use ranked data. See Milton Friedman, "The Use of Ranks to Avoid the Assumption of Normality Implicit in the Analysis of Variance," *Journal of the American Statistical Association,* Vol. 32 (December 1939), pp. 675-701.

[4] See Churchill Eisenhart, "The Assumptions Underlying the Analysis of Variance," *Biometrics,* (March 1947), pp. 3-20; William G. Cochran, "Some Consequences when the Assumptions for the Analysis of Variance are Not Satisfied," *Biometrics* (March 1947), pp. 22-38.

The Experimental Method 23

number of stores or consumers participating in the experiment. Unequal sample sizes are more often encountered in the fields of agriculture, biology, and psychology. The advantages of equal-sized samples are that the analysis is simpler and frequently less costly, and that the effect of heterogeneity of the sample variances is minimized.

Third, a *fixed-effects model* or Model I is used for analysis of variance. In a fixed-effects model, the test treatments are not randomly selected from a larger population. When the test treatments in the experiment are randomly selected from a larger population, the analysis of variance model is referred to as a *random-effects model* or Model II. When using a fixed-effects model, inferences about results cannot be generalized.[5] A fixed-effects model is usually appropriate in marketing research, since most marketing experiments can include all treatment choices which are important in terms of decision making.

SUMMARY

This chapter has discussed various types of experimental designs. Primary attention was devoted to several of the most useful informal experimental designs: before-and-after without controls, after-only with controls, and before-and-after with controls. These methods provide a measure of the treatment effect, but do not permit calculation of the potential experimental error inherent in this measurement. The concept of mathematically formal experimental designs was then introduced. Formal experimental designs do provide for the assessment of the magnitude of experimental error inherent in the test results. Part II presents four such designs which can be useful in marketing decision making. The completely randomized, randomized blocks, Latin square, and factorial designs are discussed in this part.

[5]For a more complete discussion, see B. J. Winer, *Statistical Principles in Experimental Design* (New York: McGraw-Hill Book Company, 1962), pp. 56-63.

Selected Bibliography

Banks, Seymour, *Experimentation in Marketing*. New York, McGraw-Hill Book Company, 1965. The first comprehensive book covering experimentation within the marketing area. Any marketing man interested in experimentation needs this book in his personal library.

Boyd, Harper W., and Ralph Westfall, *Marketing Research*. Homewood, Ill., Richard D. Irwin, 1964, especially Chapters 2 and 4. A standard marketing research textbook. Chapters 2 and 4 provide a general overview of the scientific approach and experimentation within the marketing area.

Campbell, Donald T., and Julian C. Stanley, "Experimental and Quasi-Experimental Designs for Research on Teaching," in N. L. Gage (ed.), *Handbook of Research on Teaching*. Chicago, Rand McNally & Co., 1963, pp. 171-246. Campbell and Stanley give a comprehensive coverage of before-and-after experiments. Internal and external validity problems are developed fully, although not within a business framework.

Cochran, William, and Gertrude Cox, *Experimental Designs*. New York, John Wiley & Sons, Inc., 1957. Perhaps the best-known experimental book used today. It does not give business examples, but has comprehensive coverage of experimentation.

Fisher, Ronald A., *The Design of Experiments*, 7th ed., Edinburgh, Scotland, Oliver and Boyd, Ltd., 1960. Fisher pioneered the development of experimentation within the area of agricultural experiments. This book explains the logic of experimentation. Unfortunately, it is not easy reading for marketing students.

Uhl, Kenneth P., "Field Experimentation: Some Problems, Pitfalls, and Perspectives," in Raymond M. Haas (ed.), *Science, Technology, and*

Marketing. American Marketing Association (Fall 1966), pp. 561-572. Uhl discusses the concepts of internal and external validity as they apply to marketing experiments. He expands Campbell's concepts to the marketing decision area.

part **II**

TECHNIQUES OF EXPERIMENTAL DESIGN

This part constitutes the heart of the book. Each of the four chapters examines a basic formal experimental design. Completely randomized designs, randomized blocks, Latin square designs, and factorial designs are presented through specific hypothetical example and generalized formula. The reader should obtain an understanding of the procedures and limitations of each design, and of the situation(s) in which each is most useful. The theme of this part is that the basic techniques of experimental design can be understood and should be known to marketing students and practitioners.

chapter 3

Completely Randomized Designs

The simplest type of formal experimental design is the completely randomized design. In this design the experimental treatments are assigned to test units on a random basis. Analysis of variance is used to determine whether treatment means differ significantly among test units. This design is most applicable to situations in which extraneous variables exert relatively equal effect on all test units. If there are large differences in extraneous variables among test units, the experimental error will be large, thus weakening the ability of the experiment to reveal significant differences among treatment means.

Since marketing phenomena are complex, extraneous variation is likely to be a significant factor in most marketing situations. For this reason the completely randomized design is seldom used by marketing researchers. However, the reader can gain an understanding of formal experimental design from this relatively simple, unstructured design. The more complex designs used by marketing researchers are more easily comprehended once the reader has become familiar with the principles underlying the completely randomized design.

ILLUSTRATION OF THE COMPLETELY RANDOMIZED DESIGN

The Jonesco Soap Company example continues to form the illustrative basis for our discussion. Mr. Jones has decided to test the effect of three types of packages on sales of JoBar. The traditional black paper wrapping, the more colorful red carton utilized in the before-and-after experiments, and a pink aluminum foil wrapper will be tested.

In the researchers' terminology, the three different packages are test treatments. Three sales territories (experimental groups) are selected. The effect of extraneous differences among experimental groups is assumed to be held constant by randomizing the assignment of treatments to each group, and by replicating the experiment four times.[1] Consequently there are twelve observations (three treatments times four replications) in this experiment. The experimental results are given in Table 3-1.

TABLE 3-1
Completely Randomized Design with 3 Treatments and 4 Replications
(Observation Y_{ij} is number of cases sold in week i by retailers exposed to treatment j)

Replications (i) (weeks)	Treatments (j)		
	1 (black wrapper)	2 (colorful carton)	3 (pink foil)
1	15	21	9
2	20	23	13
3	9	19	20
4	12	25	18
Treatment Totals	56 $\Sigma Y_{.1}$	88 $\Sigma Y_{.2}$	60 $\Sigma Y_{.3}$
Treatment Means	14 $\overline{Y}_{.1}$	22 $\overline{Y}_{.2}$	15 $\overline{Y}_{.3}$

Overall total $(\Sigma Y_{..}) = 204$; overall mean $(M) = 17$.

In this table, observation Y_{ij} is the number of cases sold in week i by retailers in the sales territory receiving treatment j. For example, Y_{23}, the second replication for treatment three, is 13 cases. The number of treatments (t) is three, and the number of replications (n) is four. To determine the mean for each treatment, we sum over the four replications of each treatment. Symbolically, this total is

$$\sum_{1}^{4} Y_{.j}$$

for a given treatment. The mean for the jth treatment, $\overline{Y}_{.j}$ is given by

---
[1] As noted in our introductory comments, this assumption may not be valid if extraneous variation is large.

Completely Randomized Designs

$$\frac{\Sigma Y_{\cdot j}}{n}$$

Analysis-of-variance techniques are used to determine whether or not the observed differences among mean values are statistically significant. In order to facilitate understanding of the analysis of variance procedures and provide for meaningful interpretation of the results of such analyses, we introduce some generalized terminology and concepts.

FIXED-EFFECTS MODEL FOR THE COMPLETELY RANDOMIZED DESIGN

In a completely randomized design, an experimental observation is given by the following linear statistical model:

$$Y_{ij} = M + T_j + E_{ij} \qquad (3\text{-}1)$$

where Y_{ij} = experimental observation of the ith replication $(i = 1, \ldots, n)$ of the jth treatment $(j = 1, \ldots, t)$
M = overall mean of experimental observations
T_j = effect of the jth treatment
E_{ij} = effect of experimental error of the jth treatment on the ith replication

The student will recall that the assumptions of the fixed-effects model are that (1) the experimental errors (E_{ij}) are independent and normally distributed about a mean of zero with a common variance; (2) $\overset{t}{\underset{j}{\Sigma}} T_j = 0$, i.e., the net effect of all treatments is zero; and (3) in this book there is an *equal number* of observations for each treatment.

Computational Formulas

In this model, the treatment effect is the difference between the treatment mean and the overall mean. Symbolically,

$$T_j = (\overline{Y}_{\cdot j} - M)$$

If a particular test treatment mean deviates from the overall mean, this indicates that the treatment being measured caused an effect different from the overall effect. The experimental error measures differences between test observations within the same treatment.

Symbolically,

$$E_{ij} = (Y_{ij} - \overline{Y}_{\cdot j})$$

These fluctuations, unexplained by the test treatments, are a measure of the random variations within each treatment in the experiment.

If we consider a single test observation in the fixed-effects model, we obtain the following expression by substituting the definitions of T_j and E_{ij} into Eq. (3-1):

$$Y_{ij} = M + (\overline{Y}_{\cdot j} - M) + (Y_{ij} - \overline{Y}_{\cdot j})$$

Subtracting the overall mean, M, from both sides of the expression, we have

$$(Y_{ij} - M) = (\overline{Y}_{\cdot j} - M) + (Y_{ij} - \overline{Y}_{\cdot j})$$

If we square both sides of the expression and sum over all the test observations, we have

$$\sum_i^n \sum_j^t (Y_{ij} - M)^2 = \sum_i^n \sum_j^t (\overline{Y}_{\cdot j} - M)^2$$

$$+ 2 \sum_i^n \sum_j^t (\overline{Y}_{\cdot j} - M)(Y_{ij} - \overline{Y}_{\cdot j}) + \sum_i^n \sum_j^t (Y_{ij} - \overline{Y}_{\cdot j})^2$$

Since

$$\sum_i^n \sum_j^t (Y_{ij} - \overline{Y}_{\cdot j}) = 0$$

the second term drops out. Also, the term $(\overline{Y}_{\cdot j} - M)^2$ is summed n times (once for each test replication). Consequently, we have the following sum of the squares for a completely randomized design:

$$\sum_i^n \sum_j^t (Y_{ij} - M)^2 = n \sum_j^t (\overline{Y}_{\cdot j} - M)^2 + \sum_i^n \sum_j^t (Y_{ij} - \overline{Y}_{\cdot j})^2$$

$$\begin{bmatrix} \text{Total sum} \\ \text{of squares} \end{bmatrix} = \begin{bmatrix} \text{treatment sum} \\ \text{of squares} \end{bmatrix} + \begin{bmatrix} \text{residual-error} \\ \text{sum of squares} \end{bmatrix} \quad (3\text{-}2)$$

For the Jonesco packaging experiment, these sums of squares are computed as follows from Table 3-1.

Completely Randomized Designs

Total Sum of Squares

$$\text{SST} = \sum_{i}^{n} \sum_{j}^{t} (Y_{ij} - M)^2 \quad (3\text{-}3)$$

$$= (15 - 17)^2 + (21 - 17)^2 + \cdots + (18 - 17)^2$$

$$= 312$$

Treatment Sum of Squares

$$\text{SSTr} = n \sum_{j}^{t} (\overline{Y}_{.j} - M)^2 \quad (3\text{-}4)$$

$$= 4[(14 - 17)^2 + (22 - 17)^2 + (15 - 17)^2]$$

$$= 152$$

Residual-Error Sum of Squares

$$\text{SSE} = \sum_{i}^{n} \sum_{j}^{t} (Y_{ij} - \overline{Y}_{.j})^2 \quad (3\text{-}5)$$

$$= (15 - 14)^2 + (21 - 22)^2 + \cdots + (18 - 15)^2$$

$$= 160$$

Degrees of Freedom

To obtain the variance estimates for the analysis-of-variance technique, each sum of squares term must be divided by the appropriate degrees of freedom. Figure 3-1 illustrates the manner in which the sums of squares deviations and appropriate degrees of freedom are partitioned in a completely randomized design.

Analysis of Variance—the F Ratio

The F ratio, named for R. A. Fisher, is a ratio of two sample estimates of the universe variance. The numerator of the ratio for the completely randomized design is the *treatment mean square,* in which differences among package treatments plus random variations are measured. The denominator is the *residual-error mean square,* which is an estimate of the

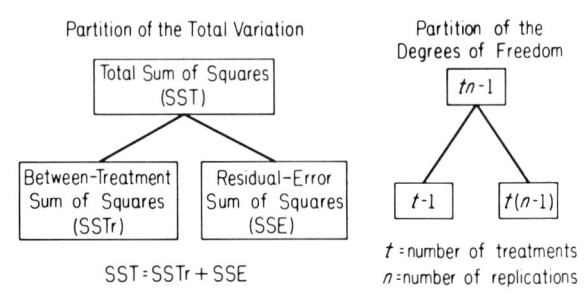

```
Partition of the Total Variation          Partition of the
                                          Degrees of Freedom

        ┌─────────────────────┐                ┌──────┐
        │ Total Sum of Squares│                │ tn-1 │
        │        (SST)        │                └──────┘
        └─────────────────────┘
           ╱              ╲                    ╱       ╲
  ┌──────────────┐  ┌──────────────┐       ┌─────┐  ┌────────┐
  │Between-Treatment│ │Residual-Error│      │ t-1 │  │ t(n-1) │
  │Sum of Squares  │ │Sum of Squares│       └─────┘  └────────┘
  │   (SSTr)       │ │    (SSE)     │
  └──────────────┘  └──────────────┘
                                          t = number of treatments
        SST = SSTr + SSE                  n = number of replications
```

Fig. 3-1. Schematic representation of completely randomized design.

random variation. If the different packages (experimental treatments) have no relative effect upon sales, the two mean-square estimates will differ only as a result of sampling error. Consequently, the F ratio will be approximately unity. As the F ratio becomes larger, the probability increases that at least two of the treatment means differ. If two treatment means differ significantly, then at least one of them has had some relative effect upon the dependent variable. These relationships are summarized in Table 3-2.

TABLE 3-2

Analysis-of-Variance Table for Completely Randomized Design

Source of Variation	Sum of Squares	Degrees of Freedom (d.f.)	Mean Square	F Ratio
Between treatments	SSTr	$t-1$	$\text{MSTr} = \dfrac{\text{SSTr}}{t-1}$	MSTr/MSE
Residual error (within treatments)	SSE	$t(n-1)$	$\text{MSE} = \dfrac{\text{SSE}}{t(n-1)}$	
Total	SST	$tn-1$		

Within the framework of this general structure, we can now see how the analysis of variance is carried out for the Jonesco packaging problem.

The results of analysis of variance are summarized in Table 3-3.

TABLE 3-3

Analysis of Variance for Completely Randomized Design

Source of Variation	Sum of Squares	d.f.	Mean Square	F
Between treatments	152	2	76.00	4.28*
Residual error (within treatments)	160	9	17.78	
Total	312	11		

*Significant at .05 level.

For the completely randomized design, the F ratio is

$$F = \frac{\text{treatment mean square}}{\text{residual-error mean square}} \qquad (3\text{-}6)$$

in which the numerator has $t - 1$ degrees of freedom (d.f.) and the denominator has $t(n - 1)$ d.f. From Table 3-3 we have

$$F = \frac{76.00}{17.78} = 4.28$$

for $(3 - 1) = 2$, and $3(4 - 1) = 9$ d.f.

Now that we have the F ratio for the Jonesco experiment, we must interpret it. That is, we must determine whether this ratio is sufficiently greater than unity to warrant a conclusion that at least one of the treatment packages has had some relative effect upon sales. This interpretation is facilitated by published tables of critical values of the F distribution in Appendix B. Degrees of freedom for the numerator are column headings. Degrees of freedom for the denominator are row headings. The intersection of a particular column and row in the body of the table gives critical values at the appropriate level of significance.

For any formal experiment, F ratios greater than these critical values occur as a result of random variation less than the critical value percent of the time. For our problem, the 5 percent critical value (for 2 and 9 d.f.) is 4.26, and the 1 percent critical value is 8.02. The experimental value we obtained, 4.28, could have arisen by chance less than 5 percent of the time, so we conclude that the results are statistically significant at the .05 level, i.e., that at least two of the treatment means differ. On the other hand, the experimental ratio is less than the 1 percent critical value, so we cannot conclude that the experimental results are significant at the .01 level.

IMPLICATIONS OF EXPERIMENT FOR MARKETING MANAGEMENT

Analysis of variance has shown (subject to a 5 percent probability of error) that packaging differences did have a relative effect upon sales of JoBar. That is, one package caused more sales than the others did. If Mr. Jones and his marketing executives are not willing to accept a 5 percent chance of being wrong, they will make no packaging changes. After all, it costs money to implement a change in package. Moreover, there were only a relatively small number of observations in the experiment.

Marketing management may conclude that, based on the experimental results, this change is not likely to increase sales in an amount sufficient to meet the costs of the change. On the other hand, if Mr. Jones and his marketing executives are willing to accept a 5 percent chance of being wrong, they will accept the conclusion that the various packages do have different effects upon sales. If this decision is made, the executives must determine which package caused the greatest amount of sales. In this case, the colorful red package (treatment 2), resulted in the largest treatment mean. Intuitively, we might conclude that the colorful package is the one to adopt, since it had the largest treatment mean. For experiments involving a larger number of treatments, and/or when results are less clear-cut, several techniques are available for more precisely determining which treatment means are significantly different.[2] A third possibility is that management might decide to obtain more information (via replication or by using a larger experiment).

This example illustrates the power of formal experimental designs as opposed to informal designs. The before-and-after designs examined in Chapter 2 did not provide a means of quantifying the potential errors inherent in observed differences in treatment effects. The assumption had to be made that these errors were of negligible magnitude. Formal experimental designs permit an assessment of the statistical significance of observed differences in treatment effects. Consequently, marketing management is given some idea of the magnitude of the risk involved in making various decisions. This additional information is certainly useful, but is the result of a more complex (and therefore more costly) experimental design. The following chapters continue to illustrate this point: more complex designs yield more informative and more reliable results, but at increasing cost. Marketing management must determine whether or not the additional information is worth the additional cost.

SUMMARY

This chapter has introduced the completely randomized experimental design. This design illustrates the principles and procedures of analysis of

---

[2]Two such tests are the Duncan Multiple Range test and the Tukey test of differences between means. See D. B. Duncan, "Multiple Range and Multiple F-tests," *Biometrics*, Vol. 11 (March 1955), pp. 1-42; J. W. Tukey, "Comparing Individual Means in the Analysis of Variance," *Biometrics*, Vol. 5 (September 1949), pp. 232-242.

Completely Randomized Designs

variance. The total sum of squared deviations is partitioned into treatment sum of squares and residual-error sum of squares. Mean squares, obtained by dividing these sums of squares by the appropriate degrees of freedom, can be ratioed to find the experimental F ratio. This ratio can be compared to critical F-ratio values at various levels of significance to provide a sound statistical basis for decision making by marketing management, provided that management accepts the basic assumptions of the design.

The completely randomized design is not often employed in marketing research because it assumes that there are no major extraneous variations within treatments. The design is useful, however, in that it facilitates understanding of the principles underlying and procedures involved in analysis of variance. The techniques of the presentation of this experimental design are continued in the following three chapters. That is, the terminology, schematic representation of variance partitions, and formulas employed—as well as the Jonesco packaging problem—are modified only to clarify the more complex designs discussed in these chapters.

PROBLEMS

1. A field interviewing company set up a completely randomized experiment to test the efficiency of its field interviewers. The number of minutes in completing a telephone interview was the dependent variable. The test results are shown in the accompanying tabulation. (a) Compute an analysis-of-variance table, with a 5 percent level of significance. [Answer: $F = 32.14$.] (b) Interpret the test results.

Replications	Interviewers			
	A	B	C	D
1	16	22	31	19
2	19	20	27	22
3	17	23	30	21
4	17	19	26	18
5	21	21	31	20

2. A rice manufacturer was testing a new form of quick-cooking rice. An experiment was set up to determine how critical the cooking time was for consumers. Twelve consumers rated three batches of the rice cooked for different time periods. The results are shown in the accompanying tabulation. (a) Compute an analysis-of-variance table. [Answer: $F = 491.60$.] (b) What would you recommend to management?

	Treatments		
Replications	A (3 min)	B (5 min)	C (7 min)
1	48	53	16
2	51	62	26
3	41	49	17
4	40	56	21

3. A mail-order company wanted to test the effect of number of days between order and delivery and number of times merchandise was returned by customers. The dependent variable is number of customers who returned the merchandise. The accompanying tabulation shows the results.

	Treatments		
Replications	A (2 days)	B (7 days)	C (14 days)
1	11	16	32
2	13	14	28

(a) Compute an analysis-of-variance table and test at a 25 percent level of significance. [Answer: $F = 34.00$.] (b) Write a brief memo to management recommending your suggested course of action.

chapter *4*

Randomized Blocks Designs

In the completely randomized design considered in the previous chapter, all sources of variation among sample results except treatment effects were assumed to be constant over all observations. A more realistic assumption in most marketing situations is that there is at least one source of extraneous or distorting variation. For situations in which there is believed to be one major source of variation, the randomized blocks design can be employed to statistically isolate that variation from the residual error. Edwards explains the value of the randomized blocks design in these terms:

> The randomized blocks design is based upon the principle of grouping experimental units into blocks. The blocks are formed with the hope that the units within each block will be more homogeneous in their response, in the absence of treatment effects, than units selected completely at random. By taking into account the differences existing between blocks in the analysis of variance, it is also anticipated that a smaller error mean square will be obtained, for the same number of observations, than if a randomized groups design had been used.[1]

Reasoning very similar to that underlying the selection of a stratified random sample rather than a simple random sample is used in selecting a randomized blocks design rather than a completely randomized design. In both decisions, a more efficient design, i.e., a smaller experimental error with a given sample size, may result from "blocking out" or separating one type of extraneous variation from the experimental error.

---

[1] Allen L. Edwards, *Experimental Design in Psychological Research*, rev. ed. (New York: Holt, Rinehart & Winston, Inc., 1962), p. 158.

ILLUSTRATION OF THE RANDOMIZED BLOCKS DESIGN

After performing the packaging experiment reported in Chapter 3, Mr. Jones realized that different regional tastes and customs could have affected the results obtained. He might like to consider the problem of packaging choice without having to worry about the effect of regional variations upon the treatment results. To achieve this objective, a randomized blocks experiment was designed.

Five different cities were selected as blocks. By using the latest census tract data, each city was divided into three approximately equal areas with similar population, income, and ethnic characteristics. This randomized blocks design, with three treatments described in Chapter 3 to be tested within five different cities is illustrated in Table 4-1. The three different geographical areas within each city are noted as A, B, and C.

TABLE 4-1
Randomized Blocks Design With 3 Treatments and 5 Blocks

Blocks Cities (i)	Treatments (j) (types of packages)		
	1 (black wrapping)	2 (red carton)	3 (pink foil)
1	A	B	C
2	A	C	B
3	C	A	B
4	B	A	C
5	C	B	A

Within each city, the three test treatments were randomly assigned to each of the three territories, using the table of random numbers given in Appendix A. The following procedure was employed. A particular row of the table was chosen. The digits were read horizontally. Since three treatments were involved, only the digits 1, 2, and 3 (corresponding to the first, second, and third treatments) were considered. The first of these digits encountered determined the treatment assigned to territory A, the second to territory B, and the third to territory C. For this experiment, territory A in city 1 was exposed to the first treatment (conventional black wrapping) during the testing period, territory C in city 2 received treatment 2, and so on. The dependent variable was again sales volume. Total sales in each test territory were tabulated for a one-week period of time in units of cases. The results of the experiment are tabulated in Table 4-2.

TABLE 4-2
Randomized Blocks Design with 3 Treatments and 5 Blocks

Block Cities (i)	Treatments (j) 1	2	3	Block Totals	Block Means
1	22	16	31	$\Sigma Y_1. = 69$	$\overline{Y}_1. = 23$
2	16	15	11	$\Sigma Y_2. = 42$	$\overline{Y}_2. = 14$
3	32	29	44	$\Sigma Y_3. = 105$	$\overline{Y}_3. = 35$
4	16	21	26	$\Sigma Y_4. = 63$	$\overline{Y}_4. = 21$
5	14	19	18	$\Sigma Y_5. = 51$	$\overline{Y}_5. = 17$
Treatment Totals	100 $\Sigma Y_{.1}$	100 $\Sigma Y_{.2}$	130 $\Sigma Y_{.3}$	330 $\Sigma Y_{..}$	
Treatment Means	20 $\overline{Y}_{.1}$	20 $\overline{Y}_{.2}$	26 $\overline{Y}_{.3}$		$M = 22$

In this table, as in Chapter 3, the observations are represented symbolically as Y_{ij}, where j is a given treatment ($j = 1, \ldots, t$) and i is a given block ($i = 1, \ldots, n$). For example, $Y_{32} = 29$. That is, the result of treatment two in city three was sales of 29 cases. To determine whether or not the observed differences in treatment means are significant, analysis of variance is employed. The fixed-effects model for the randomized blocks design is again developed in general terms before the specific problem data are analyzed.

FIXED-EFFECTS MODEL FOR RANDOMIZED BLOCKS DESIGN

A single observation in the randomized blocks design is given by

$$Y_{ij} = M + T_j + B_i + E_{ij} \tag{4-1}$$

where Y_{ij} = the j th observation in the i th block

M = overall mean

T_j = effect of the j th treatment

B_i = effect of the i th block

E_{ij} = effect of experimental error in the i th block subjected to the j th treatment.

By assumption,

(1) $\sum_{j}^{t} T_j = 0$, i.e., the net treatment effect is zero

(2) $\sum_{i}^{n} B_i = 0$, i.e., the net block effect is zero

After subtracting the mean, M, from both sides, squaring all terms, and summing, as we did in Chapter 3, the following sums of squares emerge:

$$\sum_{i}^{n}\sum_{j}^{t} (Y_{ij} - M)^2 = n \sum_{j}^{t} (\overline{Y}_{.j} - M)^2 + t \sum_{i}^{n} (\overline{Y}_{i.} - M)^2$$

$$+ \sum_{i}^{n}\sum_{j}^{t} (Y_{ij} - \overline{Y}_{.j} - \overline{Y}_{i.} + M)^2 \qquad (4\text{-}2)$$

$$\begin{bmatrix} \text{Total sum of} \\ \text{squares} \end{bmatrix} = \begin{bmatrix} \text{treatment sum} \\ \text{of squares} \end{bmatrix} + \begin{bmatrix} \text{block sum} \\ \text{of squares} \end{bmatrix} + \begin{bmatrix} \text{residual-error} \\ \text{sum of squares} \end{bmatrix}$$

For the Jonesco randomized blocks experiment, these sums of squares are as follows:

Total Sum of Squares

$$\text{SST} = \sum_{i}^{n}\sum_{j}^{t} (Y_{ij} - M)^2 \qquad (4\text{-}3)$$

$$= (22 - 22)^2 + (16 - 22)^2 + \cdots + (18 - 22)^2$$

$$= 1098$$

Treatment Sum of Squares

$$\text{SSTr} = n \sum_{j}^{t} (\overline{Y}_{.j} - M)^2 \qquad (4\text{-}4)$$

$$= 5[(20 - 22)^2 + (20 - 22)^2 + (26 - 22)^2]$$

$$= 120$$

Block Sum of Squares

$$\text{SSB} = t\sum_{i}^{n} (\overline{Y}_{i.} - M)^2 \qquad (4\text{-}5)$$

$$= 3[(23 - 22)^2 + (14 - 22)^2 + \cdots + (17 - 22)^2]$$

$$= 780$$

Residual-Error Sum of Squares

$$\text{SSE} = \sum_{i}^{n}\sum_{j}^{t} (Y_{ij} - \overline{Y}_{.j} - \overline{Y}_{i.} + M)^2 \qquad (4\text{-}6)$$

$$= (22 - 20 - 23 + 22)^2 + (16 - 20 - 23 + 22)^2 + \cdots$$

$$+ (18 - 26 - 17 + 22)^2$$

$$= 198$$

To obtain the variance estimates (mean squares) which comprise the F ratio, each sum-of-squares term is divided by the appropriate degrees of freedom. Figure 4-1 illustrates the partition of the total sum of squares and total degrees of freedom in the randomized blocks design.

Partition of the Total Variation

Total Sum of Squares (SST)
├── Between-Block Sum of Squares (SSB)
└── Within-Block Sum of Squares
    ├── Between-Treatment Sum of Squares (SSTr)
    └── Residual-Error Sum of Squares (SSE)

SST = SSB + SSTr + SSE

Partition of the Degrees of Freedom

$tn - 1$
├── $n - 1$
└── $n(t - 1)$
    ├── $t - 1$
    └── $(n - 1)(t - 1)$

t = number of treatments
n = number of blocks

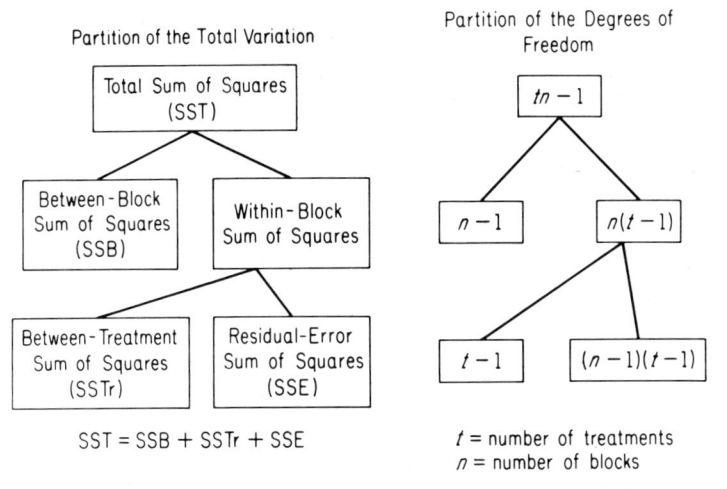

Fig. 4-1. Schematic representation of randomized blocks design.

The procedure for analysis of variance in the randomized blocks design is summarized in Table 4-3.

TABLE 4-3
Analysis-of-Variance Table for Randomized Blocks Design

Source of Variation	Sum of Squares	d.f.	Mean Square	F Ratio
Between blocks	SSB	$n-1$	$MSB = \dfrac{SSB}{n-1}$	MSB/MSE
Between treatments	SSTr	$t-1$	$MSTr = \dfrac{SSTr}{t-1}$	MSTr/MSE
Residual error	SSE	$(n-1)(t-1)$	$MSE = \dfrac{SSE}{(n-1)(t-1)}$	
Total	SST	$tn-1$		

The use of this generalized framework permits the efficient analysis of our packaging experiment in different cities.

The test results are summarized in Table 4-4.

TABLE 4-4
Analysis of Variance for Randomized Blocks Design

Source of Variation	Sum of Squares	d.f	Mean Square	F
Between treatments	120	2	60.00	2.42*
Between blocks	780	4	195.00	7.88[†]
Residual error	198	8	24.75	
Total	1,098	14		

*Significant at .25 level.
[†]Significant at .01 level.

Since the critical F ratio for 2 and 8 degrees of freedom at the 5 percent level of significance is 4.66, the F ratio is not statistically significant at the 5 percent level. At a higher level of risk, say the 25 percent level, the F ratio is statistically significant. Note also the statistical significance of the between-blocks variance. This significance indicates that consumers' JoBar purchasing habits did vary among the cities tested.

IMPLICATIONS OF EXPERIMENT FOR MARKETING MANAGEMENT

Traditionally, statisticians have not given much credence to results which were not significant at the 5 percent level or less. Marketing management, however, must make some decision regardless of experimental results. In this case, if management's decision is to change packages, the risk involved in assuming that the packages are significantly different is high. For this reason management might want to adopt a higher alpha-risk level. Alternatively, the experiment could be replicated, perhaps on a larger scale, to increase the precision of the information obtained.

The use of formal experimental designs permits a calculation of the relative efficiency (decrease in size of experimental error with a given sample size) of the randomized blocks design as opposed to the completely randomized design. The formula for this calculation is given by:[2]

$$\text{Relative efficiency} = \frac{(b-1)B + b(t-1)E}{(bt-1)E} \quad (4\text{-}7)$$

where B = block mean square
E = residual-error mean square
b = number of blocks
t = number of treatments

$$\text{R.E.} = \frac{(5-1)\ 195.00 + 5\ (3-1)\ 24.75}{[(5)(3) - 1]\ 24.75}$$

$$= \frac{780 + 247.5}{346.5}$$

$$= \frac{1002.75}{346.5}$$

$$= 2.89$$

Because of the large-block mean square relative to the experimental-error mean square, as indicated by the significant F ratio, the randomized blocks design is almost three times as efficient as a completely randomized design would be in the same situation. Further efficiency might be gained by using Latin square or factorial designs, which are discussed in subsequent chapters.

SUMMARY

The randomized blocks design is an appropriate experimental technique when one major source of extraneous variation is present. By grouping or "blocking" the test observations, this source of variation can be re-

[2]See Bernard Ostle, *Statistics in Research,* 2d ed. (Ames, Iowa; Iowa State University Press, 1963), pp. 374-375.

moved from the residual error. The underlying logic of the design is that test units within blocks should be more homogeneous than test units in different blocks. This design is generally more efficient for marketing research than the completely randomized design, because sources of extraneous variation are usually present in marketing situations. When there is more than one source of extraneous variation, the Latin square design may be more efficient than the randomized blocks design.

PROBLEMS

1. A manufacturer was considering changing its existing package. Three alternative packages were tested, along with the present package. The sales of all package alternatives were tested in supermarkets, drugstores, and variety stores over a period of one month. The test results are shown in the accompanying tabulation. Analyze and interpret the sales test results. [Answer: $F_t = 14.35, F_b = 0.91$.]

	Treatments			
Blocks	A (present package)	B	C	D
Supermarkets . . .	76	68	88	80
Drugstores	74	70	102	86
Variety stores . . .	66	66	92	92

2. A professor in a business school tested the effectiveness of three teaching techniques. Fifteen students who were divided into five business majors rated the effectiveness of the techniques. The results are shown in the accompanying tabulation. (a) Compute the analysis-of-variance table. (b) Interpret the results. [Answer: $F_t = 1.36, F_b = 10.19$.]

Blocks (business majors)	Treatments		
	A (lecture)	B (group cases)	C (business game)
Accounting	11	10	9
Finance	32	28	30
Marketing	30	72	48
Management . . .	42	50	43
Economics	10	15	20

Randomized Blocks Designs

3. A consumer magazine wanted to measure the effect that different subscription price offerings had upon sales of new magazine subscriptions. Three different price treatments were tested in a randomized blocks design. The three different blocks of people were (1) housewives, (2) college students, and (3) businessmen. A total of 250 people were sent letters with each of the three treatment price offerings within each block. The dependent variable was the number of new magazine subscriptions. The test results are shown in the accompanying tabulation. (a) Compute the analysis-

	Treatments		
Blocks	100 Percent of Normal Price	80 Percent of Normal Price	60 Percent of Normal Price
Housewives	96	114	165
College students	90	110	163
Businessmen . . .	114	136	182

of-variance table. [Answer: F_b = 975.00 and F_t = 113.25.] (b) Evaluate the sensitivity of the three blocks of people to price changes of the consumer magazine. Write a brief recommendation to management in terms of pricing strategy.

chapter 5

Latin Square Designs

In the preceding chapter we examined the randomized blocks design, which allows statistical control of one major source of extraneous variation. The Latin square design permits statistical control of two noninteracting sources of extraneous variation, in addition to treatments, which might affect the dependent variable. This design has many potential uses in marketing research, particularly in retailing, where differences among test stores, geographical regions, and time periods can be statistically controlled.

ILLUSTRATION OF THE LATIN SQUARE DESIGN

In the randomized blocks design discussed in Chapter 4, Mr. Jones controlled the effect of regional variations in JoBar sales by using cities in various regions. Within cities, the test treatments (different types of packages) were assigned to test stores at random. After examining the results of this experiment, Mr. Jones felt that an additional variable—type of store—might have been another major extraneous factor affecting sales of JoBar.

To control for both regional variations and type of store variations, a Latin square experiment was designed. In the Latin square design it is conventional to think of the two extraneous sources of variation as forming the rows and columns of a table. Treatment effects are then assigned to cells in the table randomly, subject to the restriction that each treatment appears once only in each row and each column of the table. Consequently the number of rows, columns, and treatments must be equal, a restriction not necessary in the randomized blocks design. It is from this feature of its design that the Latin square derives its name.

Mr. Jones was interested in the effects of three different types of packages upon sales of JoBar. Also, three different store types were con-

Latin Square Designs

sidered important: supermarkets, drugstores, and convenience stores. Three geographically separated test cities were selected. Thus, the experiment became a 3 X 3 (read "three by three") Latin square. This design is illustrated in the upper-left segment of Table 5-1. In this design, the rows are types of stores, columns represent different test cities, and the treatments are the three package designs. Treatment A is the traditional black package, treatment B is the colorful red carton, and treatment C is the pastel pink foil wrapper. This table also gives selected Latin squares of various sizes which can be used as "starting points" for other Latin square designs.[1]

TABLE 5-1
Selected Latin Squares for Randomization

```
      3 x 3                          4 x 4
    A  B  C                      A  B  C  D
    B  C  A                      B  C  D  A
    C  A  B                      C  D  A  B
                                 D  A  B  C

        5 x 5                         6 x 6
    A  B  C  D  E              A  B  C  D  E  F
    B  C  D  E  A              B  C  D  E  F  A
    C  D  E  A  B              C  D  E  F  A  B
    D  E  A  B  C              D  E  F  A  B  C
    E  A  B  C  D              E  F  A  B  C  D
                               F  A  B  C  D  E
```

The randomization procedure described in Chapter 4 can be applied to these selected squares to obtain a Latin square design for experiments of three to six treatments. For the present experiment, the columns were randomized in the following order of random numbers: 2, 3, 1. The following Latin square emerges:

```
    2  3  1
    B  C  A
    C  A  B
    A  B  C
```

The rows were than randomized by means of random numbers generated in the following order: 1, 3, 2. The finalized Latin square for this

---

[1]For a more complete discussion, see Allen L. Edwards, *Experimental Design in Psychological Research*, rev. ed. (New York: Holt, Rinehart & Winston, Inc., 1962), pp. 258-259.

experiment thus has the following appearance:

```
1  B  C  A
3  A  B  C
2  C  A  B
```

Consequently, for this experiment, treatment B (the colorful red package) will be assigned to supermarkets in city one, to drugstores in city two, and to convenience stores in city three. Table 5-2 presents the complete Latin square to be used in this experiment.

TABLE 5-2
Latin Square Design for Jonesco Experiment

Rows (type of store)	Columns (cities) 1	2	3
1 (supermarket)	B	C	A
2 (drugstore)	A	B	C
3 (convenience store)	C	A	B

The results obtained from conducting the Jonesco experiment for a two-week period are given in Table 5-3. The observation, Y_{ij}, represents the number of cases of JoBar sold by store type i in city j during the specified monthly time period. For example, Y_{13} is 32 cases. To determine whether the observed differences in row, column, and treatment

TABLE 5-3
Results of Jonesco Latin Square Experiment

Rows (i)	Columns (j) 1	2	3	Row Totals	Row Means
1	36	52	32	$\Sigma Y_{1.} = 120$	$\overline{Y}_{1.} = 40$
2	23	27	40	$\Sigma Y_{2.} = 90$	$\overline{Y}_{2.} = 30$
3	70	62	27	$\Sigma Y_{3.} = 159$	$\overline{Y}_{3.} = 53$
Column totals	129 $\Sigma Y_{.1}$	141 $\Sigma Y_{.2}$	99 $\Sigma Y_{.3}$	$\Sigma Y_{..} = 369$	
Column means	43 $\overline{Y}_{.1}$	47 $\overline{Y}_{.2}$	33 $\overline{Y}_{.3}$		$M = 41$
Treatments (k)	A	B	C		
Totals	117 $\Sigma Y_{..(1)}$	90 $\Sigma Y_{..(2)}$	162 $\Sigma Y_{..(3)}$		
Means	39 $\overline{Y}_{..(1)}$	30 $\overline{Y}_{..(2)}$	54 $\overline{Y}_{..(3)}$		

Latin Square Designs

means are significant, analysis-of-variance techniques were employed. The general fixed-effects model for the Latin square is developed to facilitate this analysis.

FIXED-EFFECTS MODEL FOR LATIN SQUARE DESIGN

A test observation in a Latin square design is given by the linear statistical model

$$Y_{ij(k)} = M + R_i + C_j + T_k + E_{ij(k)} \quad (5\text{-}1)$$

where M = overall mean
R_i = effect of ith row
C_j = effect of jth column
T_k = effect of kth treatment
$E_{ij(k)}$ = effect of experimental error in the ith row and jth column subjected to the kth treatment

$$i = j = k = 1, \ldots, t$$

By assumption,

$$\sum_i^t R_i = 0 \quad \sum_j^t C_j = 0 \quad \text{and} \quad \sum_k^t T_k = 0$$

that is, the net effect of the various rows, columns, and treatments is zero.

After subtracting the mean, M, from both sides of Eq. 5-1, squaring all terms, and summing, the following sum of squares emerge:

$$\sum_i^t \sum_j^t (Y_{ij(k)} - M)^2 = t \sum_i^t (\overline{Y}_{i\cdot} - M)^2 + t \sum_j^t (\overline{Y}_{\cdot j} - M)^2$$

$$+ t \sum_k^t (\overline{Y}_{\cdot\cdot(k)} - M)^2 + \sum_i^t \sum_j^t (Y_{ij(k)} - \overline{Y}_{i\cdot} - \overline{Y}_{\cdot j} - \overline{Y}_{\cdot\cdot(k)} + 2M)^2$$

(5-2)

$$\begin{bmatrix} \text{Total sum of} \\ \text{squares} \end{bmatrix} = \begin{bmatrix} \text{row sum} \\ \text{of squares} \end{bmatrix} + \begin{bmatrix} \text{column sum} \\ \text{of squares} \end{bmatrix} + \begin{bmatrix} \text{treatment sum} \\ \text{of squares} \end{bmatrix}$$

$$+ \begin{bmatrix} \text{residual-error} \\ \text{sum of squares} \end{bmatrix}$$

For the present experiment, these sums of squares are as follows.

Total Sum of Squares

$$\text{SST} = \sum_{i}^{t}\sum_{j}^{t}(Y_{ij(k)} - M)^2 \qquad (5\text{-}3)$$

$$= (36 - 41)^2 + (52 - 41)^2 + \cdots + (27 - 41)^2$$
$$= 2226$$

Row Sum of Squares

$$\text{SSR} = t\sum_{i}^{t}(\overline{Y}_{i.} - M)^2 \qquad (5\text{-}4)$$

$$= 3[(40 - 41)^2 + (30 - 41)^2 + (53 - 41)^2]$$
$$= 798$$

Column Sum of Squares

$$\text{SSC} = t\sum_{j}^{t}(\overline{Y}_{.j} - M)^2 \qquad (5\text{-}5)$$

$$= 3[(43 - 41)^2 + (47 - 41)^2 + (33 - 41)^2]$$
$$= 312$$

Treatment Sum of Squares

$$\text{SSTr} = t\sum_{k}^{t}(\overline{Y}_{..(k)} - M)^2 \qquad (5\text{-}6)$$

$$= 3[(39 - 41)^2 + (30 - 41)^2 + (54 - 41)^2]$$
$$= 882$$

Residual-Error Sum of Squares

$$\text{SSE} = \sum_{i}^{t}\sum_{j}^{t}(Y_{ij(k)} - \overline{Y}_{i.} - \overline{Y}_{.j} - \overline{Y}_{..(k)} + 2M)^2 \qquad (5\text{-}7)$$

$$= [36 - 40 - 43 - 30 + 2(41)]^2$$
$$+ [52 - 40 - 47 - 54 + 2(41)]^2$$
$$+ \cdots + [27 - 53 - 33 - 30 + 2(41)]^2$$
$$= 234$$

ANALYSIS OF VARIANCE FOR THE LATIN SQUARE DESIGN

To obtain the mean squares which comprise the F ratio, each sum of squares term is divided by the appropriate degrees of freedom. Figure 5-1 illustrates the partition of the total sum of squares and appropriate degrees of freedom for the Latin square design.

Partition of the Total Variation

- Total Sum of Squares (SST)
  - Between-Row Sum of Squares (SSR)
  - Within-Row Sum of Squares
    - Between-Column Sum of Squares (SSC)
    - Within-Row-and-Column Sum of Squares
      - Between-Treatment Sum of Squares (SSTr)
      - Residual-Error Sum of Squares (SSE)

SST = SSR + SSC + SSTr + SSC

Partition of the Degrees of Freedom

- $t^2 - 1$
  - $t - 1$
  - $t^2 - t$
    - $t - 1$
    - $t^2 - 2t + 1$
      - $t - 1$
      - $(t - 1)(t - 2)$

t = number of treatments, rows, and columns

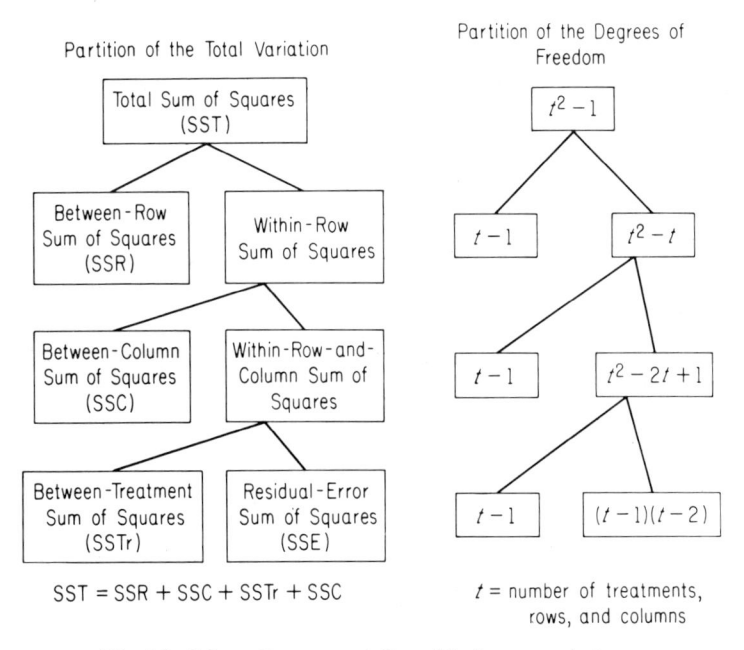

Fig. 5-1. Schematic representation of Latin square design.

The generalized analysis of variance procedure for the Latin square design is shown in Table 5-4. Both Fig. 5-1 and Table 5-4 are applicable to the analysis of variance for any size Latin square.

TABLE 5-4
Analysis-of-Variance Table for Latin Square Design

Source of Variation	Sum of Squares	d.f.	Mean Square	F Ratio
Between rows	SSR	$t-1$	$MSR = \dfrac{SSR}{t-1}$	MSR/MSE
Between columns ..	SSC	$t-1$	$MSC = \dfrac{SSC}{t-1}$	MSC/MSE
Between treatments .	SSTr	$t-1$	$MSTr = \dfrac{SSTr}{t-1}$	MSTr/MSE
Residual error	SSE	$(t-1)(t-2)$	$MSE = \dfrac{SSE}{(t-1)(t-2)}$	
Total	SST	$t^2 - 1$		

This generalized framework facilitates the computations necessary to the analysis of the present problem. The test results are summarized in Table 5-5.

TABLE 5-5
Analysis of Variance of Results of Latin Square Experiment

Source of Variation	Sum of Squares	d.f.	Mean Square	F Ratio
Between treatments...	882	2	441	3.77*
Between rows	798	2	399	3.41*
Between columns	312	2	156	1.33
Residual error	234	2	117	
Total	2,226	8		

*Significant at .25 level.

None of the mean variations obtained in the present experiment is statistically significant at less than the .25 level. Thus there is one chance in four that these differences could have been the result of random variations in the sample data.

IMPLICATIONS OF EXPERIMENT FOR MARKETING MANAGEMENT

The pink foil wrapper, treatment C, had the highest mean sales rate (54 cases per period). If Mr. Jones is willing to accept a rather high risk of being wrong, he will adopt the pink foil wrapper. This decision might be advisable, since some action must be taken. If Mr. Jones concludes that a 25 percent probability of error is too high, he will probably decide to continue using the traditional black package, since a change in package designs would involve additional expenditure. A third possibility is that Mr. Jones might recognize that an experiment involving only nine observations may not be sufficiently comprehensive to be reliable. This possibility is reflected in the small number of degrees of freedom appropriate to each sum-of-squares component. Mr. Jones might therefore decide to replicate the experiment to increase the reliability of the experimental results.

The experiment could be replicated in the same stores and cities over several months. This procedure would increase the number of observations, thereby reducing the impact of any one particular random fluctuation in the data. Replication, however, poses the potential danger of *carryover effects*. That is, the observations obtained in a given month might be distorted or biased by the effect of the experiment in previous months. For example, some consumers might notice that a given store which carried the colorful red carton (treatment B) in a previous month now stocks the pink foil wrapper (treatment C). These consumers might then purchase JoBar in the pink foil wrapper—not because of its attractiveness but simply because they noticed the change. This carryover effect can be controlled by using a modified Latin square design known as the *double-changeover* design. In this design, each treatment directly follows each of the other treatments once and only once. Consequently, when a carryover effect is present, the treatment means are adjusted to reflect this influence. If the carryover effect is not significant, the design can be analyzed as two conventional Latin squares.[2]

Another refinement of the Latin square design which might be useful to marketing management is the *Graeco-Latin Square* design. This design permits the statistical isolation of the effects of three noninteracting extraneous variables or the analysis of two types of treatments while isolating the effects of two noninteracting extraneous variables. For example, Mr. Jones might want to test different package sizes of JoBar as well as different wrappings. This could be done with a Graeco-Latin square design by superimposing a Latin square of package-size treatments denoted by Greek letters (α, β, γ) upon the conventional Latin square experiment described in this chapter. In this design, each Greek letter also occurs once

---

[2] See Edwards, *op. cit.*, pp. 274–276 for a more complete discussion.

and only once in each row and column, and once and only once with each Latin letter. Table 5-6 demonstrates a 3 × 3 Graeco-Latin square design.

TABLE 5-6
Illustration of a Graeco-Latin
Square Design

Rows	Columns		
	1	2	3
1	αB	βC	γA
2	βA	γB	αC
3	γC	αA	βB

The Graeco-Latin square design reduces the degrees of freedom in the error term for a given sample size, but does permit statistical control of an additional variable.[3] Marketing management must determine whether the gain in information is worth the additional cost of implementing this design. Indeed, it is the task of marketing management to make decisions about the value of experimental research in general. This task involves comparisons among alternative designs.

COMPARISON OF ALTERNATIVE EXPERIMENTAL DESIGNS

Marketing management is usually interested in solving a particular problem in the most efficient manner possible. Efficiency in research design is a function of the situation about which information is desired. The more complex the situation, the greater the need for a more complex design. This point can be illustrated by reviewing the designs considered for the Jonesco packaging problem. To enhance the clarity of the discussion, the characteristics of the completely randomized, randomized blocks, and Latin square designs are briefly summarized:

1. The *completely randomized design* is appropriate to a situation in which the population to be estimated is fairly homogeneous except for treatment effects. This is usually the cheapest and easiest formal experimental design.

2. The *randomized blocks design* is appropriate for estimat-

---

[3]See Seymour Banks, *Experimentation in Marketing* (New York: McGraw-Hill Book Company, 1965), pp. 168–179, for a more complete discussion and an example of the use of the Graeco-Latin square design in marketing research.

Latin Square Designs

ing parameters in a population which has one major source of uncontrollable variation in addition to treatment effects.

3. The *Latin square design* is used to statistically isolate two sources of uncontrollable variation in addition to treatment effects. The Latin square design assumes no interactions between treatments and extraneous variations, nor between the two sources of variation. Also, the number of row, columns, and treatments must be equal.

In Chapter 3, the Jonesco packaging problem was researched using a completely randomized design to test the effect on sales of three different packages of JoBar. It was assumed that no major source of extraneous variation would systematically bias the error term. Since Mr. Jones felt that geographic differences might result in such a bias, a randomized blocks design was employed, as discussed in Chapter 4. Another potential source of extraneous variation in sales results, differences in type of store, lead to the use of a Latin square design to statistically remove from the error term the effects of both geographic location and type of store.

These changes in the experimental design were expected to increase the efficiency of the research. Given equal-sized samples for each design, such a gain could only be achieved if the variations removed from the error term were of sufficient magnitude to overcome the loss of degrees of freedom in the residual error. That is, for a given sample size the effect of chance receives fewer independent measurements in the more complex designs. Consequently, the impact of a particular random fluctuation upon the error term is greater, thus reducing the significance of treatment differences. Table 5-7 shows the degrees of freedom which each design has in its error term, given that each experiment has three treatments ($t = 3$), and is replicated three times or has three blocks ($n = 3$).

TABLE 5-7

Degree of Freedom in Residual-Error Sum of Squares for Three Different Experimental Designs

Experimental Design	Generalized d.f. in Residual Error	d.f. where $t = 3$, and $n = 3$
Completely randomized design .	$t(n-1)$	6
Randomized blocks	$(n-1)(t-1)$	4
Latin square	$(t-1)(t-2)$	2

The reader can see from Table 5-7 that if a population is in fact homogeneous, treatment effects in the Latin square experiment described in Table 5-7 would have to be approximately twice as large as those of a completely randomized design to be of equal statistical significance. On the other hand, if the population is not homogeneous, greater statistical significance can be achieved with a given sample size by using a more complex design. The relative efficiency of various designs in a given situation can be calculated to determine whether a more complex design is justified. The formulas for these calculations are given by Ostle.[4]

The efficiency of the present Latin square design is calculated relative to a completely randomized design, and to a randomized blocks design in which store types are used as blocks. For the completely randomized design, the formula is

$$\text{Relative efficiency} = \frac{R + C + (t - 1)E}{(t + 1)E} \qquad (5\text{-}8)$$

where R = row mean square
C = column mean square
E = error mean square
t = number of rows, columns, and treatments

The data are obtained from Table 5-5.

$$\text{R.E.} = \frac{399 + 156 + 2(117)}{4(117)}$$

$$= 1.66$$

The formula for the efficiency of the Latin square design relative to a randomized blocks design in which the effects of store types (row effects) are blocked out is

$$\text{Relative efficiency} = \frac{R + (t - 1)E}{tE} \qquad (5\text{-}9)$$

where the terms are as defined above.
Applying the data from Table 5-5, we have

$$\text{R.E.} = \frac{399 + 2(117)}{3(117)}$$

$$= 1.80$$

These calculations show that the Latin square design employed in the Jonesco packaging situation was approximately $1^{2/3}$ times as efficient as a

[4]Bernard Ostle, *Statistics in Research*, 2d ed. (Ames, Iowa: Iowa State University Press, 1963), p. 414.

Latin Square Designs

completely randomized design or a randomized blocks design using store types as blocks would have been in this situation. Marketing management must determine whether this increased efficiency is worth the additional cost of implementing a Latin square design in any given situation. In marketing, the more complex designs are generally considered to be worthwhile because of the heterogeneity of marketing populations. This heterogenity is illustrated by the concept of *market segmentation*, in which an attempt is made to subdivide a given market into more homogeneous segments.[5]

SUMMARY

The Latin square design enables the researcher to statistically isolate two sources of major extraneous variation from the residual error. This is a valuable ability in marketing, an area in which conditions generally are complex. Consequently, variations of the Latin square design are frequently employed in marketing research. The additional efficiency gained from the use of the Latin square design in a particular situation must be weighed against the additional cost and technical expertise involved in implementing it. Further efficiency can be gained from the use of a factorial design in conjunction with the other formal designs presented. Factorial designs are discussed in Chapter 6.

PROBLEMS

1. A company wanted to measure the effect of some alternative promotions upon sales. A 4 × 4 Latin square was set up for the test.

Time Periods	Stores			
	1	2	3	4
1	B	A	C	D
2	D	C	B	A
3	A	B	D	C
4	C	D	A	B

[5]For excellent discussions of the concept of market segmentation, see Philip Kotler, *Marketing Management: Analysis, Planning and Control* (Englewood Cliffs, N. J.: Prentice-Hall, Inc., 1967), Chapter 3; and W. R. Smith, "Product Differentiation and Market Segmentation as Alternative Marketing Strategies," *Journal of Marketing* (July 1956), pp. 3-8.

The test treatments were:

Treatment A = no promotion
B = shelf point of purchase
C = free samples with demonstrator
D = special end display

The test results are shown in the accompanying tabulation. (a) Compute analysis-of-variance table, using a 5 percent level of significance. [Answers: $F_t = 1.37$, $F_r = 1.16$, and $F_c = 2.37$] (b) What would you recommend to the promotion manager?

Time Periods	Stores			
	1	2	3	4
1	14	8	17	9
2	18	16	21	13
3	14	16	25	17
4	10	12	17	29

2. An advertising agency was interested in finding out how effective price dealing was for a major coffee client. A 3 × 3 Latin square experiment was set up to measure the effect of three alternative price deals upon coffee sales of the client.

Time Periods	Stores		
	1	2	3
1	B	A	C
2	C	B	A
3	A	C	B

Treatment A = 15 cents off regular price
B = 10 cents off regular price
C = 5 cents off regular price

The test results are shown in the accompanying tabulation. Compute the analysis of variance and analyze the effectiveness of price dealings for coffee. [Answers: $F_t = 2.33$, $F_c = 0.58$, and $F_r = 4.08$]

Time Periods	Stores		
	1	2	3
1	48	66	51
2	63	63	72
3	69	63	72

Latin Square Designs

3. A food manufacturer had nine people rate three different varieties of a new food product developed in its test kitchens. A 3 × 3 Latin square experiment was used.

Ethnic Groups	Ages		
	25-35	36-50	Over 50
Irish	C	B	A
Italian	A	C	B
English	B	A	C

The three test treatments of the new food product were labeled A, B, and C. The test results are shown in the accompanying tabulation. (a) Com-

Ethnic Groups	Ages		
	25-35	36-50	Over 50
Irish	29	41	32
Italian	36	30	39
English	40	31	36

pute an analysis-of-variance table. [Answer: $F_t = 2.71$, $F_r = .14$, and $F_c = .14$.] (b) Discuss the possibility that the ratings of the products are a function of age and ethnic backgrounds. (c) Given the knowledge in this experiment, how would you design an experiment to repeat the same test?

chapter **6**

Factorial Designs

In the preceding chapters, several different research designs have been utilized to measure the effect of different types or levels of one particular treatment upon the dependent variable. In many marketing situations, it is desirable to test the effect of two or more treatments at various levels. An experiment of this type is particularly appropriate when there is reason to believe that the treatments might *interact* to produce an effect upon the dependent variable which neither treatment alone would produce.

Factorial designs provide the means for conducting experiments under these circumstances. It is customary to denote the size of a factorial experiment as an x^n factorial experiment, where n is the number of treatments or factors and x the number of levels of each treatment. Thus a 2^3 factorial experiment is one which employs two levels of each of three different treatments. Factorial experiments may be used with any of the three formal experimental designs previously discussed, or with more complicated experimental designs. In this chapter, we will examine a 2^2 factorial design within a completely randomized design.

ILLUSTRATION OF THE FACTORIAL DESIGN

Mr. Jones has been testing the effect of different package designs upon sales of JoBar. The results of these experiments have not consistently demonstrated the superiority of any of the package designs tested. Mr. Jones feels that more conclusive results might be obtained if the effect of point-of-purchase promotional activity (shelf signs, wall posters, etc.) is examined along with the effect of different packages. Accordingly, the old package will be tested against the colorful red carton, both with and without point-of-purchase promotional material.

Factorial Designs

A completely randomized design (as described in Chapter 3) will be the basis for our factorial experiment. There are two levels of each of the two treatments (package change and point-of-purchase promotion) for a total of four treatments. The old package is designated A_1, the new

TABLE 6-1
2 × 2 Factorial Design

		B_1 Point-of- Purchase Material	B_2 No Point-of- Purchase Material
A_1	Old Package	A_1B_1	A_1B_2
A_2	New Package	A_2B_1	A_2B_2

package A_2; the presence of certain shelf advertisements is B_1, the absence of point-of-purchase promotional material is B_2. These four treatments were randomly assigned to 20 stores so that the experiment was replicated five times during a one month test period. The factorial design and test results are given in Tables 6-1 and 6-2 respectively.

TABLE 6-2
Results of Jonesco 2^2 Factorial Experiment

Replications (stores) (i)	Treatments (j)				
	A_1		A_2		
	B_1	B_2	B_1	B_2	
1	21	19	18	12	
2	23	21	16	10	
3	22	20	23	9	
4	21	19	21	13	
5	18	21	17	16	
Treatment Totals.....	105 $\Sigma Y_{.1}$	100 $\Sigma Y_{.2}$	95 $\Sigma Y_{.3}$	60 $\Sigma Y_{.4}$	360 $\Sigma Y_{..}$
Treatment Means.....	21 $\overline{Y}_{.1}$	20 $\overline{Y}_{.2}$	19 $\overline{Y}_{.3}$	12 $\overline{Y}_{.4}$	18 M

In this table the entry Y_{ij} denotes the number of cases of JoBar sold in store i ($i = 1, \ldots, 5$) receiving treatment j ($j = 1, \ldots, 4$).

COMPUTATIONS FOR JONESCO FACTORIAL EXPERIMENT

Initially, the analysis of factorial experimental results follows the procedures for the analysis of the completely randomized design. As described in Chapter 3, the fixed-effects model is employed. Sums of squares are calculated and divided by appropriate degrees of freedom to obtain the mean squares from which the F ratio is calculated.

Total Sum of Squares

$$\text{SST} = \sum_{i}^{n} \sum_{j}^{t} (Y_{ij} - M)$$
$$= (21 - 18)^2 + (19 - 18)^2 + \cdots + (16 - 18)^2$$
$$= 332 \qquad [3\text{-}3]$$

Treatment Sum of Squares

$$\text{SSTr} = n \sum_{j}^{t} (\overline{Y}_{.j} - M)^2$$
$$= 5[(21 - 18)^2 + (20 - 18)^2 + (19 - 18)^2 + (12 - 18)^2]$$
$$= 250 \qquad [3\text{-}4]$$

Residual-Error Sum of Squares

$$\text{SSE} = \sum_{i}^{n} \sum_{j}^{t} (Y_{ij} - \overline{Y}_{.j})^2$$
$$= (21 - 21)^2 + (19 - 20)^2 + \cdots + (16 - 12)^2$$
$$= 82 \qquad [3\text{-}5]$$

Analysis of Variance

Table 6-3 presents the analysis of variance for the initial phase of the factorial experiment.

Factorial Designs

TABLE 6-3
Initial Analysis of Variance for Factorial Experiment

Source of Variation	Sum of Squares	d.f.	Mean Square	F Ratio
Between treatments	250	3	83.33	16.26*
Residual error	82	16	5.13	
Total	332	19		

*Significant at .01 level.

The critical F value for 3 and 16 d.f. is 5.29 at the .01 level of significance. The experimental F ratio thus indicates a significant difference between at least two of the treatment effects. Since two factors were involved in the experiment, it is necessary to further examine the experimental results to determine the treatment effects upon sales of JoBar with greater precision.

PARTITION OF THE TREATMENT SUM OF SQUARES

The increased precision of the factorial design results from the partition or division of the total treatment effect into parts attributable to each factor, and to the interaction between factors. Symbolically, for the two-factor case,

$$T_j = A_k + B_l + (AB)_{kl} \tag{6-1}$$

where T_j = net treatment effect of the jth treatment
A_k = treatment effect of the kth level of factor A
B_l = treatment effect of the lth level of factor B
$(AB)_{kl}$ = treatment effect of the interaction of the kth level of factor A and the lth level of factor B

The total number of treatments t is equal to the number of factor A treatments (denoted by a) times the number of factor B treatments (denoted by b). That is, $t = ab$.

Since the experiment is replicated n times, the treatment sum of squares is given by

$$n \sum_{j}^{t} (\overline{Y}_{.j} - M)^2$$

as derived in Eq. (3-4). It can be shown (by rather laborious algebraic manipulation) that this sum of squares has the following composition:

$$n \sum_{j}^{t} (\overline{Y}_{.j} - M)^2 = bn \sum_{k}^{a} (\overline{Y}_{Ak} - M)^2 + an \sum_{l}^{b} (\overline{Y}_{Bl} - M)^2$$

$$+ n \sum_{k}^{a} \sum_{l}^{b} (\overline{Y}_{.j} - \overline{Y}_{Ak} - \overline{Y}_{Bl} + M)^2 \qquad (6\text{-}2)$$

$$\begin{bmatrix} \text{Treatment} \\ \text{sum of squares} \end{bmatrix} = \begin{bmatrix} \text{treatment A} \\ \text{sum of squares} \end{bmatrix} + \begin{bmatrix} \text{treatment B} \\ \text{sum of squares} \end{bmatrix}$$

$$+ \begin{bmatrix} \text{interaction AB} \\ \text{sum of squares} \end{bmatrix}$$

The data required to compute these sums of squares of the Jonesco experiment are summarized in Table 6-4.

TABLE 6-4
Summary of Jonesco Factorial Experiment Results

Package Design	Point-of-Purchase		Package Design Totals	Package Design Means
	B_1	B_2		
A_1	105	100	$\Sigma A_1 = 205$	$\overline{YA}_1 = 20.5$
A_2	95	60	$\Sigma A_2 = 155$	$\overline{YA}_2 = 15.5$
Point-of-purchase Totals	200 ΣB_1	160 ΣB_2	$\Sigma Y_{..} = 360$	
Point-of-purchase Mean	20.0 $\overline{YB}_1$	16.0 $\overline{YB}_2$		$M = 18$

For the present experiment, these sums of squares are calculated as follows:

Treatment A Sum of Squares

$$\text{SSTa} = bn \sum_{k}^{a} (\overline{Y}_{Ak} - M)^2$$

$$= (2)(5)[(20.5 - 18)^2 + (15.5 - 18)^2]$$

$$= 125 \qquad (6\text{-}3)$$

Factorial Designs

Treatment B Sum of Squares

$$\text{SSTb} = an \sum_{l}^{b} (\overline{Y}_{Bl} - M)^2$$

$$= (2)(5)[(20 - 18)^2 + (16 - 18)^2]$$

$$= 80 \tag{6-4}$$

Treatment Interaction Sum of Squares

$$\text{SSTab} = n \sum_{k}^{a} \sum_{l}^{b} (\overline{Y}_{.j} - \overline{Y}_{Ak} - \overline{Y}_{Bl} + M)^2$$

$$= 5[(21 - 20.5 - 20 + 18)^2 + (20 - 20.5 - 16 + 18)^2$$
$$+ (19 - 15.5 - 20 + 18)^2 + (12 - 15.5 - 16 + 18)^2]$$

$$= 45 \tag{6-5}$$

Check

$$250 = 125 + 80 + 45$$

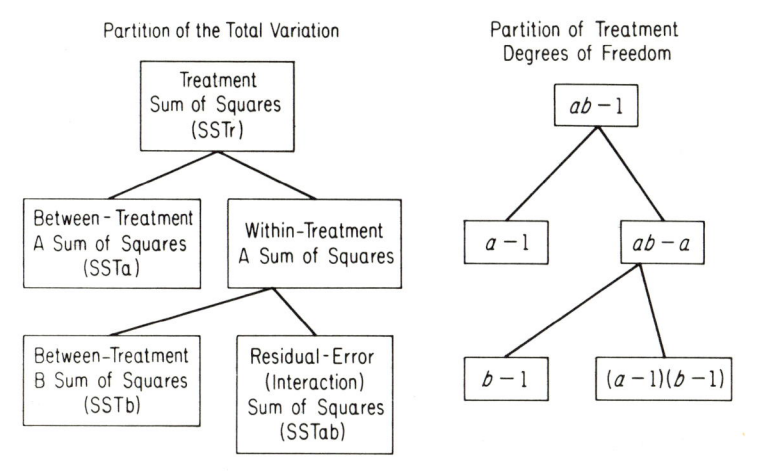

$$\text{SSTr} = \text{SSTa} + \text{SSTb} + \text{SSTab}$$

a = number of levels of factor A
b = number of levels of factor B
$t = ab$

Fig. 6-1. Schematic representation of factorial design (two-factor case).

Each of these parts of the treatment sum of squares has 1 d.f. in the two-factor case. The complete model of sums-of-squares components and degrees of freedom for each component is shown schematically in Fig. 6-1. The generalized analysis-of-variance procedure for the two-factor factorial design within a completely randomized design is given in Table 6-5.

TABLE 6-5
Analysis-of-Variance Procedure for Two-Factor Factorial Design
(Within a completely randomized design)

Source of Variation	Sum of Squares	d. f.	Mean Square	F Ratio
Treatment A	SSTa	$a - 1$	$MSa = \dfrac{SSTa}{a-1}$	MSa/MSE
Treatment B	SSTb	$b - 1$	$MSb = \dfrac{SSTb}{b-1}$	MSb/MSE
Interaction AB	SSTab	$(a-1)(b-1)$	$MSab = \dfrac{SSTab}{(a-1)(b-1)}$	MSab/MSE
Residual error	SSE	$ab(n-1)$	$MSE = \dfrac{SSE}{ab(n-1)}$	
Total	SST	$abn - 1$		

These generalized procedures provide an analytical framework for assessing the results of the Jonesco factorial experiment. Now we are ready to determine the statistical significance of the complete factorial experiment and to examine the managerial implications of this experiment.

IMPLICATIONS OF THE FACTORIAL EXPERIMENT FOR MARKETING MANAGEMENT

The complete analysis of variance of the factorial experiment is presented in Table 6-6. The interpretation of these figures provides a basis for managerial decision making.

Since the critical F value for 1 and 16 d.f. is 8.53 for the .01 significance level, the experimental F ratios indicate that all three treatments did produce statistically significant results. The F ratio for treatment A indicates that the two packages had different effects on sales. The old package was more effective, since it had the larger mean sales rate. Point-of-

TABLE 6-6
Complete Analysis of Variance of the Jonesco Factorial Experiment
(Within a completely randomized design)

Source of Variation	Sum of Squares	d. f.	Mean Square	F Ratio
Treatment A	125	1	125.00	24.39*
Treatment B	80	1	80.00	15.61*
Interaction AB	45	1	45.00	8.78*
Residual error	82	16	5.13	
Total	332	19		

*Significant of .01 level

purchase promotional material also significantly affected sales in a positive manner. Mean sales were 16.0 cases per month without point-of-purchase activity, and 20.0 when point-of-purchase was used.

In addition, the interaction of package type and point-of-purchase activity was significant. This relationship can best be shown by graphical means. Figure 6-2 presents a graph of mean sales rate for treatment A at each level of treatment B.

Figure 6-2 shows that, for the old package (treatment A_1), the mean sales rate was 21.0 when point-of-purchase materials were employed (treat-

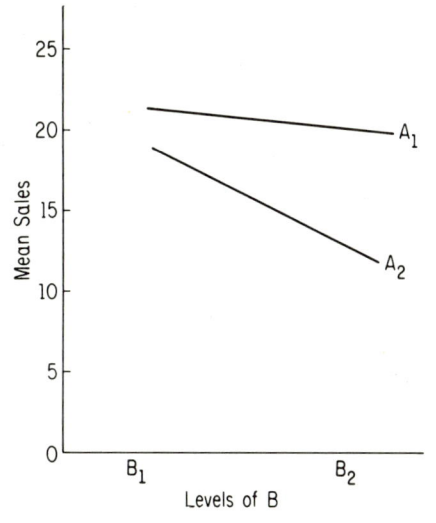

Fig. 6-2. Mean sales of treatment A at each level of treatment B.

ment B_1). The new package (treatment A_2) had mean sales of 19.0 for treatment B_1. The deletion of point-of-purchase promotion (treatment B_2) caused mean sales rates of both package types to decline, but the decline was significantly more severe for the new package. Sales of the old package declined to 20 cases, while sales of the new package declined to 12 cases. Thus, the interaction effect was that point-of-purchase promotional activity was more important to sales of the new (and therefore unfamiliar) package than it was to the regular package.

This experiment illustrates the potential value of the factorial experimental design to marketing management. In many marketing situations the interactions of several variables may significantly affect sales results. The other experimental designs discussed provide no measure of these possible interactions. The factorial design can be expanded to encompass a number of such interactions, and thus is a research tool which can provide additional meaningful information to marketing management. Factorial designs hold great potential for marketing research in experimenting with several marketing-mix elements at the same time,—e.g., different price levels and different amounts of advertising.

It is appropriate to mention at this point another technique that can be employed to increase the precision of experimental results. This technique is termed *covariance analysis*. It can be used in conjunction with any of the four experimental designs discussed. Covariance analysis is basically a procedure for adjusting observational data before analysis of variance to statistically control for known differences among observations. For example, on our packaging experiments in stores, we have assumed that conditions in a given store are constant for the duration of the experiment. However, if total store receipts vary from day to day, differences in sales of various packages of JoBar may be distorted by the fluctuations in total sales. If marketing management believes that this distortion might seriously bias the experimental results, covariance analysis can be employed to adjust actual observations of JoBar sales to a common total-receipts base.[1]

There are numerous other statistical techniques which are useful to marketing management. For the most part such techniques represent refinements and extensions of the basic concepts of experimentation discussed in this book. These techniques are used to perform experi-

[1] For more complete discussions, see Bernard Ostle, *Statistics in Research*, 2d ed. (Ames, Iowa: Iowa State University Press, 1963), pp. 437-465; Paul E. Green and Donald S. Tull, "Co-Variance Analysis in Marketing Experimentation," *Journal of Advertising Research*, (June 1966), pp. 45-53.

ments more efficiently, to obtain more precise results, and to compensate for missing data. The reader who has carefully addressed himself to the concepts presented here has a foundation upon which to build a working knowledge of such techniques and of experimentation in general. The reader is urged to obtain this knowledge by becoming acquainted with some of the standard works in the field. A selection of such works is noted in the bibliography at the end of each part.

SUMMARY

The factorial experimental design is examined in this chapter. This design permits comparisons among various levels of two or more interacting factors. The design can be used within the framework of other experimental designs. Factorial experimental designs provide precise information about treatment effects by partitioning the treatment sum of squares into its various components.

This additional information is not without cost, however. Increased benefit must be weighed against increased expense. That is, the marketing manager must compare the various experimental designs and plan his experiment so that efficient use is made of them. Efficient experimental planning and design are the result of knowledge and experience. Many refinements and extentions of the basic techniques described in this book are available to marketing management. To assist the reader in acquiring additional knowledge about experimentation in marketing, Part III presents summaries of a number of actual experiments in the decision areas of marketing. A discussion of the managerial aspects of experimentation concludes the book.

PROBLEMS

1. A market research firm was attempting to decrease its mail sample nonresponse. A 2 × 2 factorial design test was conducted to measure the number of mail responses. The factorial design was:

Color of questionnaire
    A_1 = white
    A_2 = green
Type of postage
    B_1 = regular
    B_2 = airmail

The completely randomized design was replicated five times for the four different treatments. The dependent variable was the total number of mail-sample responses. The accompanying tabulation shows the results.
(a) Compute analysis of variance at the 5 percent significance level.
(b) Assuming the cost of questionnaire color is the same for both white and green, and that regular postage is 6 cents and airmail 10 cents, what would you recommend in terms of alternatives? [Answer: $F_t = 0.17$, $F_a = 0.26$, $F_b = 0.26$, and $F_{ab} = 0.00$.]

Replications	A_1		A_2	
	B_1	B_2	B_1	B_2
1	21	20	9	19
2	12	28	17	26
3	23	13	11	15
4	15	16	22	12
5	14	18	16	13

2. A national company tested a 2 × 2 factorial design with two different levels of two media expenditures.
The expenses were:
Treatment A_1 = high magazine expense
Treatment A_2 = low magazine expense
Treatment B_1 = high TV expense
Treatment B_2 = low TV expense
The experiment was replicated three times, so that twelve different metropolitan markets were used as the test units. The results in sales units of

Replications	A_1		A_2	
	B_1	B_2	B_1	B_2
1	22	26	20	18
2	29	21	24	19
3	30	19	25	23

$1,000 are shown in the accompanying tabulation. Analyze what the results mean. [Answer: $F_t = 2.29$, $F_a = 2.35$, $F_b = 4.17$, and $F_{ab} = 0.26$.]

Selected Bibliography

Edwards, Allen L., *Experimental Design in Psychological Research,* rev. ed. New York: Holt, Rinehart & Winston, Inc., 1962. Gives a detailed description of formal experimental designs. He relates the use of experimentation to decisions within the area of psychology.

Cox, Keith K., "The Role of Experimentation in the Information System of a Retailer," in L. George Smith (ed.), *Reflections on Progress in Marketing.* American Marketing Association (December 1964), pp. 383-391. Describes how a Latin square design, a randomized blocks, and a factorial design can be utilized in obtaining relevant information for a retailer.

Freund, John, Paul Livermore, and Irwin Miller, *Manual of Experimental Statistics.* Englewood Cliffs, N. J.: Prentice-Hall, Inc., 1960. This manual does not help the beginning student to learn about experimentation. However, it is a valuable library book for quick and easy reference in planning and executing experimental research.

Jessen, Raymond J., "A Switch-Over Experimental Design to Measure Advertising Effect," *Journal of Advertising Research* (March 1961), pp. 15-22. Jessen's article shows how a switch-over design can be used in measuring advertising effectiveness. It is an excellent example of building a more complex experimental design for a particular marketing decision area.

Ostle, Bernard, *Statistics in Research* 2d ed. Ames, Iowa: Iowa State University Press, 1963. Presented in greater statistical depth than is Edwards' book. Ostle is a good reference for the practitioner.

Uhl, Kenneth P., "Factorial Design—Aid to Management," *Journal of Marketing* (January 1962), pp. 62-66. Uhl gives an in-store factorial design which is typical of many experiments in this decision area.

part *III*

APPLICATION OF EXPERIMENTATION TO MARKETING DECISION MAKING

This part presents actual experimental work in the marketing field, and discusses the managerial aspects of such applications. Chapters 7 and 8 describe experiments in the functional marketing areas of pricing, distribution, product strategy, and promotion. Chapter 9 reviews the managerial implications of these applications, and summarizes the uses and limitations of experimental design in marketing research. The theme of this part is that experimentation has demonstrated value to marketing management, and that experimentation will become increasingly useful in the future.

chapter 7

Experiments in Distribution, Pricing, and Product Policies

This chapter discusses actual experiments in the decision areas of distribution, pricing and product design. The purpose of this discussion is to demonstrate the application of experimentation to marketing problems. The current "state of the art" is indicated by the fact that four of the six experiments described are before-and-after type designs. The other two experiments are Latin square designs. These six experiments are, in the opinion of the authors, a representative cross-sampling of experimental research in these areas of marketing. From a study of these experiments, the reader can gain insight into the usefulness of experimentation in the areas of distribution, pricing, and product design.

DISTRIBUTION EXPERIMENTS

In the decision area of distribution, two different experiments are reported. Sevin measured the effect that changing methods of distribution to unprofitable accounts had upon net profit contribution.[1] Cox measured the effect that alternative shelf space had upon the sales of food products.[2]

Sevin Alternative Channels Experiment

A detailed cost analysis indicated that a national manufacturer had many small and unprofitable customers. The present system of the com-

[1] Charles H. Sevin, *Marketing Productivity Analysis* (New York: McGraw-Hill Book Company, 1965), pp. 96–98.
[2] Keith Cox, "The Responsiveness of Food Sales to Supermarket Shelf Space Changes," *Journal of Marketing Research* (May 1964), pp. 63–67.

78   Application of Experimentation to Marketing Decision Making

pany was to distribute directly to all customers through company-owned branches and a field sales force. Alternative distribution choices which management wanted to consider were (1) to switch the distribution of small unprofitable customers from direct selling through company branches to mail orders, and (2) to switch the distribution of small unprofitable customers from direct selling to wholesale distributors. The two alternatives were tested along with the present distribution system, using the following treatment alternatives:

Treatment 1: Small, unprofitable customers–mail order
Treatment 2: Small, unprofitable customers–wholesale distributor
Treatment 3: Small, unprofitable customers–company branches (present system)

Three groups of territories that were as similar as possible with regard to such factors as urban-rural proportions of the population and economic characteristics of the areas were selected for the experiment. The dependent variable was net profit contribution. That is, the null hypothesis tested was that alternative distribution methods do not affect the net profit contribution of the sales territories. A before-and-after with control design was carried out, as illustrated in Fig. 7-1.

Experimental Distribution 1 (Mail Order)	Net Profit Contribution Before Change (Y_1)	→	Net Profit Contribution After Change (Y_2)
Experimental Distribution 2 (Wholesale Distributors)	Net Profit Contribution Before Change (Z_1)	→	Net Profit Contribution After Change (Z_2)
Control Distribution (Present System)	Net Profit Contribution Before Change (X_1)	→	Net Profit Contribution After No Change (X_2)

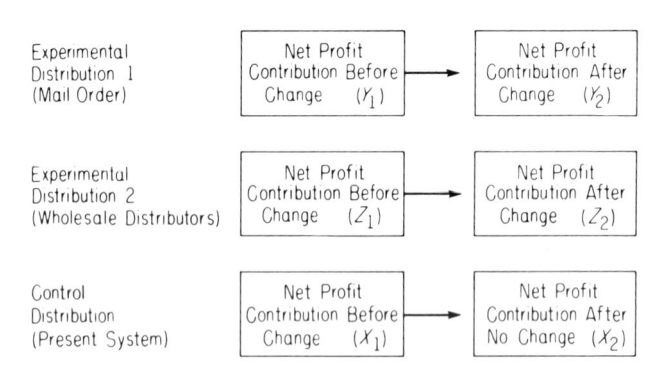

Fig. 7-1. Sevin before-and-after with control design.

The treatment effect of switching to mail-order distribution for small accounts from direct selling was

$$(Y_2 - Y_1) - (X_2 - X_1)$$

The treatment effect of switching to wholesale distributors for small accounts from direct selling was

$$(Z_2 - Z_1) - (X_2 - X_1)$$

The results of the experiment at the end of a year are shown in Table 7-1.

TABLE 7-1
Experimental Results of Changes in Distribution Methods on Net Profit Contribution

Treatments	Net Profit Contribution (percent)			Treatment Effect
	Before	After	Change	
Experimental distribution 1 (mail order)	100.0	111.8	+11.8	9.5
Experimental distribution 2 (wholesale distributors)	100.0	121.4	+21.4	19.1
Control distribution (present system)	100.0	102.3	+2.3	

Table 7-1 shows that there was a 9.5 percent increase (11.8 − 2.3) in dollar profit contribution in the territories in which small unprofitable customers were serviced through mail orders, as compared to the existing system of selling through company branches. However, there was a 19.1 percent increase (21.4 − 2.3) in dollar profit contribution when the small unprofitable customers were turned over to wholesale distributors. As a result of these experiments, marketing management adopted a national policy of allowing wholesale distributors to service the small unprofitable accounts in those areas where suitable distributors were available.

Cox Shelf-Space Experiment

In the area of food distribution, a decision important to both food manufacturers and supermarket retailers is the allocation of shelf space to product categories within supermarkets. The object of this experiment was to measure the relationship between shelf space and product sales. Four product categories selected for the experiment were hominy, baking soda,

80   Application of Experimentation to Marketing Decision Making

Tang, and powdered coffee cream. We will limit the discussion in this book to the hominy experiment.

The null hypothesis advanced was that there was no significant relationship between the amount of shelf space given to hominy (independent variable) and total unit sales of hominy (dependent variable). A 6 × 6 Latin square design was selected for this experiment, since the potential extraneous variations among supermarkets and over time were thought to be significant. Six test stores were chosen for the experiment, which lasted six weeks (six time periods of one week). The six shelf treatments (number of shelf spaces) for the hominy experiment were:

Treatment A: 4 shelf spaces
Treatment B: 6 shelf spaces
Treatment C: 8 shelf spaces
Treatment D: 10 shelf spaces
Treatment E: 12 shelf spaces
Treatment F: 14 shelf spaces

The actual Latin square design employed is given in Table 7-2. Note the characteristics of this Latin square design. Each store is exposed to each treatment once over the life of the experiment. In each week, all six treatments are tested.

TABLE 7-2
Cox 6 × 6 Latin Square Design for Shelf-Space Experiment

Stores	Weeks					
	1	2	3	4	5	6
1	E	D	A	C	B	F
2	F	B	C	E	A	D
3	C	F	B	A	D	E
4	A	E	D	B	F	C
5	B	C	F	D	E	A
6	D	A	E	F	C	B

In setting up the experimental test to measure the relationship between shelf space and product sales of hominy, all other variations besides treatment, store, and time differences had to be controlled. The shelf level employed in each store at the start of the experiment was maintained throughout the experiment. Prices of hominy remained constant, and no sales-promotional materials or advertising of hominy were used. The results of the experiment (unit sales of hominy) are given in Table 7-3.

TABLE 7-3
Results of Cox 6 × 6 Latin Square Shelf-Space Experiment

Stores	Weeks						
	1	2	3	4	5	6	Totals
1	140	150	71	111	121	127	720
2	131	126	130	188	133	154	862
3	67	94	49	93	112	161	576
4	109	134	96	123	127	84	673
5	58	71	59	62	49	27	326
6	37	36	52	58	38	51	272
Totals...	542	611	457	635	580	604	3,429

Treatment Totals

A	B	C	D	E	F
469	528	501	611	724	596

Table 7-3 indicates that 140 cans of hominy were sold in store 1 during the first test week when twelve shelf spaces (treatment E) were used. Other values are interpreted in analogous manner. Applying the formulas from Chapter 5, the analysis of variance in Table 7-4 was computed:

TABLE 7-4
Analysis of Variance for Cox Hominy Experiment

Source of Variation	d. f.	Sum of Squares	Mean Square	F Ratio
Rows (stores)	5	44,455.9	8,891.2	25.00*
Columns (weeks)....	5	3,450.3	690.1	1.94
Treatments (shelf spaces)	5	7,130.9	1,426.2	4.01
Linear regression....	1	4,230.7	4,230.7	11.89*
Deviation from linearity	4	2,900.2	725.1	2.04
Residual error	20	7,113.7	355.7	
Total	35	62,150.8		

*Significant at .01 level.

In analyzing the results, both an analysis-of-variance test and a regression-analysis test were used to measure the effect of the treatment shelf spaces upon hominy sales. The regression-analysis test divides the treatment sum of squares and treatment degrees of freedom into two sub-

82 Application of Experimentation to Marketing Decision Making

groups.[3] The null hypothesis tested was that there was no linear relationship between shelf space and hominy sales. Using a predetermined 5 percent level of significance with 1 and 20 d. f., the critical F ratio is 4.35. Since the actual F ratio was 11.89, the null hypothesis was rejected and the alternative hypothesis was accepted that there was a significant relationship between amount of shelf space and hominy sales. In general, allocating additional shelf space resulted in higher sales of the product.

PRICING EXPERIMENTS

Price is another important marketing-mix variable which affects dependent variables (e.g., sales, market share) of interest to marketing management. We shall examine two pricing experiments. The Hawkins study is a report of a before-and-after without controls measurement on the effect of changes in the retail price of a product upon the product's market share.[4] Grieg, Strand, and Larzelere measured the effect of retail price reductions on sales of dehydrated potato products, using a 4 × 4 Latin square design.[5]

Hawkins Before-and-After Without Controls Pricing Experiment

In the study reported by Hawkins, the retail prices of several grocery products were changed from one period to the next in one supermarket chain. We shall examine the results of the experiment on pie-crust mix. The null hypothesis was that price increases of two cents would have no effect upon the market shares of leading brands of pie-crust mix. The price of each of the two leading brands stocked by the chain was raised two cents at the beginning of period two. This increase constituted the experimental treatment. The prices of the other three brands were held constant throughout the two periods. Market share was measured by store audits at the ends of both periods. This research design is illustrated in Fig. 7-2.

---

[3] For a greater technical discussion of the regression analysis test within an analysis-of-variance framework, see Bernard Ostle, *Statistics in Research*, 2d ed. (Ames, Iowa: Iowa State University Press, 1963), pp. 312–315.
[4] E. W. Hawkins, "Methods of Estimating Demand," *Journal of Marketing* (April 1957), pp. 428–438.
[5] W. S. Grieg, F. O. Strand, and H. E. Larzelere, "Relative Retail Sales and Elasticity of Demand for Dehydrated Mashed Potato Products," Agricultural Economics Department Cooperative Extension Service, Michigan State University, East Lansing (July 1958).

```
┌──────────────────┐      ┌──────────────────┐
│  Market Share    │      │  Market Share    │
│ Before Treatment │─────▶│ After Treatment  │
│      (Y₁)        │      │      (Y₂)        │
└──────────────────┘      └──────────────────┘
```

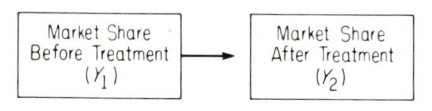

Y_1 = market share of each brand in period 1
Y_2 = market share of each brand in period 2

Fig. 7-2. Hawkins before-and-after without control design.

The treatment effect, therefore, is given by

$$Y_2 - Y_1$$

for each brand. The results of this experiment are presented in Table 7-5.

TABLE 7-5

Results of Hawkins Before-and-After Pricing Experiment

Brand of Pie-Crust Mix	Retail Price (cents) Period 1	Retail Price (cents) Period 2	Share of Market (percent) Period 1	Share of Market (percent) Period 2	Change
A	14	16	12.8	9.0	−3.8
B	14	16	59.8	47.0	−12.8
C	14	14	10.5	16.1	5.6
D	15	15	9.5	18.9	9.4
E	15	15	7.4	9.0	1.6
			100.0	100.0	0.0

As we might expect from the study of elementary economics, the increase in price for brands A and B had an inverse effect upon the respective market shares of those brands. Brand A's share dropped 3.8 percent; brand B's decrease was 12.8 percent. The market shares of brands C, D, and E increased. Ostensibly, marketing management should conclude that price increases reduce market share.

However, the before-and-after without controls design has serious limitations. It provides no method of measuring the potentially distorting impact of numerous extraneous factors (e.g., weather, competitors' actions, changes in promotional policies) upon market share. We must assume that such variables affected each brand's market share equally. Moreover, this design affords no measure of the effect of random variations in the sample data. Consequently, generalizations about the effect of price increases under other conditions are subject to significant error possibilities. The Latin square design discussed below takes such problems into account.

Grieg Latin Square Pricing Experiment

Price reductions of 10, 20, and 30 percent from the base price of a dehydrated-potato product constituted the independent variables in this experiment. Specifically, the treatments were:

Treatment A: Base price for each produce = 100%
Treatment B: Base price reduced 10% = 90%
Treatment C: Base price reduced 20% = 80%
Treatment D: Base price reduced 30% = 70%

The null hypothesis was that such price changes would have no effect upon sales of the products. Thus the dependent variable was sales of the potato products, measured in number of packages sold per week period.

The Latin square design employed to test the hypothesis had four different grocery stores as columns, and four different two-week periods as rows. The actual Latin square utilized is shown in Table 7-6.

TABLE 7-6
Grieg 4 X 4 Latin Square Design for Potato-Pricing Experiment

Time Periods	Stores			
	1	2	3	4
1	A	B	C	D
2	B	D	A	C
3	C	A	D	B
4	D	C	B	A

This design statistically isolated the effects of store and time variations upon sales of the potato products. Other potential extraneous effects, such as differences in promotional activity, consumer characteristics or weather, were assumed to influence sales on a random basis and were measured by the experimental error. The results of the experiment are shown in Table 7-7.

The reader can see from the data that sales did increase as the prices of the products were reduced. This result is to be expected from elementary demand theory. An analysis of variance was performed to determine the statistical significance of this trend, and the significance of store or time period effects upon sales. This analysis is summarized in Table 7-8.

At the 5 percent level of significance with 3 and 6 d.f., the null hypothesis that price reductions would have no effect on sales of dehydrated-potato products was rejected. Sales were significantly increased by lowering the price of the product. Of course, management would want to

TABLE 7-7
Results of Grieg Latin Square Pricing Experiment
(Total sales of packages of a dehydrated-potato product)

Time Periods	Stores 1	Stores 2	Stores 3	Stores 4	Total
1	68	86	75	60	289
2	82	127	59	57	325
3	97	56	79	53	285
4	108	105	63	51	327
Total	355	374	276	221	1,226

Treatment Totals

A	B	C	D
234	284	334	374

Note: Values were interpolated from Graph 5, p. 15 of the report.

determine whether the sales increase was large enough to compensate for the decrease in per-unit revenue associated with the price cut. The effect of different stores upon sales was also significant. The Latin square design statistically removed this influence, thus providing a more precise estimate of the effect of price reductions upon sales.

TABLE 7-8
Analysis of Variance for Potato-Pricing Experiment

Source of Variation	Sum of Squares	d. f.	Mean Squares	F Ratio
Rows (time)	2,626.00	3	875.33	1.31
Columns (stores)	11,364.50	3	3,788.17	5.68*
Treatments (price)	14,523.50	3	4,841.00	7.26*
Residual error	4,000.00	6	666.67	
Total	32,514.00	15		

*Significant at .05 level.

PRODUCT EXPERIMENTS

Two experiments are reported within the area of product strategy. Muhler et al., in conducting the Crest stannous fluoride experiments, measured the effect that stannous fluoride had upon tooth decay.[6] Allison and Uhl measured the effect that brand labeling had upon consumer taste preference for beer.[7]

Muhler Toothpaste Experiment

This experiment was conducted to test the effect of a toothpaste containing stannous fluoride upon tooth cavities. Cavities were measured in the experiment by examining students at Indiana University and recording their decayed, missing, and filled surfaces. The students were divided into nine classes based upon their previous cavity experience. Within each class, the students were assigned randomly to the test group or to the control group. The treatments were:

Treatment 1: Dentifrice with stannous fluoride (SnF_2)
(test group)
Treatment 2: Dentifrice with no stannous fluoride
(control group)

The dependent variable was average number of cavities. A before-and-after with control design was used to test the null hypothesis that the addition of stannous fluoride had no effect upon cavity formation. Figure 7-3 illustrates the experimental design employed.

```
Test Groups      [Cavities Before      →   [Cavities After
                  Experiment (Y_1)]         Using SnF_2  (Y_2)]

Control Groups   [Cavities Before      →   [Cavities After Not
                  Experiment (X_1)]         Using SnF_2  (X_2)]
```

Treatment effect = $(Y_2 - Y_1) - (X_2 - X_1)$

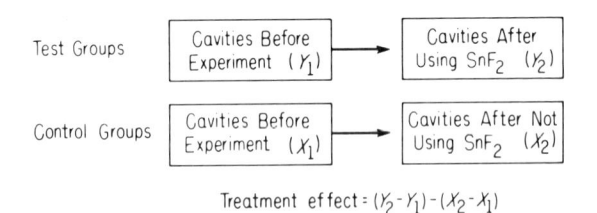

Fig. 7-3. Muhler before-and-after with control design.

The two groups of 359 students were reexamined six months after the test began. The test results, in terms of the average number of cavities counted before and after the experiment, are given in Table 7-9.

[6] Joseph C. Muhler, Arthur W. Radike, William H. Nebergall, and Harry G. Day, "The Effect of a Stannous Fluoride-Containing Dentifrice on Dental Caries in Adults," *Journal of Dental Research* (February 1956), pp. 49-53.

[7] Ralph I. Allison and Kenneth P. Uhl, "Influence of Beer Brand Identification of Taste Perception," *Journal of Marketing Research* (August 1964), pp. 36-39.

TABLE 7-9
Results of Stannous Fluoride Experiment upon Tooth Decay

	Before Experiment	After Experiment	Change	Treatment Effect
Test group	26.90	27.57	0.67	−.68
Control group	27.70	29.05	1.35	

The results showed that college students who used the stannous fluoride dentifrice experienced approximately a 50 percent reduction in tooth decay during a six-month test period as compared to the student control group. Because of this and similar test results conducted at the University of Indiana in cooperation with the Procter & Gamble Company, the American Dental Association awarded its seal of approval to "Crest" toothpaste, which used stannous fluoride in the toothpaste.

Allison and Uhl Brand Preference Experiment

This experiment tested the effect that beer brand labeling had upon consumer preference for beer. The two alternative treatments (independent variables) were:

Treatment 1: Unlabeled beer
Treatment 2: Labeled beer

A test group of 326 males who drank beer at least three times a week was randomly selected in the market area. Each participant in the experiment was given a six-pack of unlabeled beer. Each six-pack contained three brands of beer which were randomly placed in the pack. Every bottle was rated by the participant using a general rating scale. Thus the dependent variable was the quality rating which each bottle received.

The empty unlabeled beer and rating tags were picked up one week after the original distribution, and a new six-pack was left. This time, the bottles were properly labeled by brand. These bottles and tags were picked up one week later. This before-and-after without controls design is illustrated in Fig. 7-4.

Test Groups: Unlabeled Beer Preferences (Y_1) → Labeled Beer Preferences (Y_2)

Treatment effect = $Y_2 - Y_1$

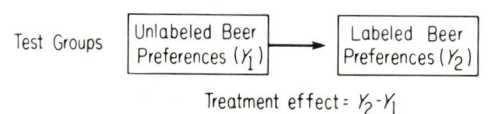

Fig. 7-4. Allison before-and-after without control experiment.

The test results, in terms of the general rating scale, are given in Table 7-10.

TABLE 7-10
Results of Allison Comparison Taste Test for Beer

Brand	Beer Test Unlabeled	Beer Test Labeled	Change
A	65	71	+6
B	64	73	+9
C	63	68	+5
D	63	77	+14
E	63	67	+4

The test results show that all five brands in the labeled test were more highly rated than were the same brands in the "blind" tests. These findings suggest that physical product differences are not the only factors that influence the success or failure of various brands in the marketplace.

SUMMARY

This chapter has presented six actual experiments in the marketing decision areas of distribution, pricing, and product policy. Four of these experiments were before-and-after designs: Sevin on alternative distribution methods, Hawkins on price changes, Muhler on product modification, and Allison and Uhl on branding. Each of these experiments provided useful information for management, but did not measure the magnitude of error inherent in the information. Two Latin square designs— Cox on shelf space and Grieg on pricing—were also examined. Both of these experiments gave management an estimate of the accuracy of the results obtained. For this reason, the use of formal experimental designs in actual marketing research is expected to increase. The following chapter presents examples of experimental work in the promotional area, in which wider use has been made of formal experimental designs.

PROBLEMS

1. Assume that the research director wants to use a formal experimental design in the Sevin distribution experiment. (a) What research design would you choose? (b) Evaluate the strengths and weaknesses of your choice.

2. In Cox's shelf-space experiment, a Latin square design was employed. In an additional research project within the same decision area, the marketing manager recommended that a randomized blocks design be used. (a) Physically set up your experiment within a randomized blocks design. (b) Evaluate the marketing manager's choice of design.

3. Explain some of the major control problems that researchers would have faced if they used a formal experimental design in conducting the Muhler toothpaste experiment.

chapter 8

Experiments in Promotion

Perhaps more experiments have been conducted in the area of promotion than in all three of the other marketing-decision areas combined. This chapter reviews six promotion experiments which employed several types of experimental designs. These experiments tend to refute the traditional belief that the effectiveness of promotional appeals cannot be measured.

JENSSEN TELEVISION COMMERCIAL EXPERIMENT

This experiment measured the effect of different TV commercials upon actual sales of a product.[1] Samples of consumers were used as test participants who were about to enter a shopping-center supermarket to do their weekly shopping. The different treatments were:

Treatment 1: No exposure to TV advertising message (control)
Treatment 2: Exposure to TV advertising message "alpha"
Treatment 3: Exposure to TV advertising message "beta"

All three groups of test consumers were interviewed just before entering a large Los Angeles supermarket. The control group of consumers was given a gift packet of ten different cents-off coupons. These coupons could be used only in the test supermarket, and only on that particular day. One of the coupons was for product "X." Another group of consumers were given the same gift packet after viewing four TV commercials in a trailer parked in the shopping center. One of the advertisements was "alpha," a TV ad for "X," the product under study. A third group of consumers followed the same procedure, except that they were exposed to "beta," a different TV ad for "X." Figure 8-1 illustrates this design.

[1]Ward J. Jenssen, "Sales Effect of TV, Radio, and Print Advertising," *Journal of Advertising Research* (June 1966), pp. 2-7.

Experiments in Promotion

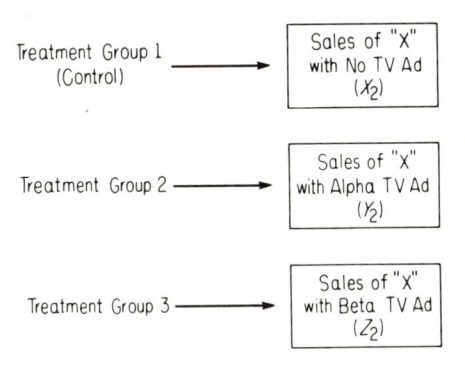

```
Treatment Group 1  ──▶  Sales of "X"
   (Control)              with No TV Ad
                             (X₂)

Treatment Group 2  ──▶  Sales of "X"
                         with Alpha TV Ad
                             (Y₂)

Treatment Group 3  ──▶  Sales of "X"
                         with Beta TV Ad
                             (Z₂)
```

Treatment effect of alpha = $Y_2 - X_2$
Treatment effect of beta = $Z_2 - X_2$

Fig. 8-1. Jenssen after-only with control design.

Since consumers in all three groups were similar in all relevant respects, and all received identical assortments of various cents-off coupons, the different rates of redemption sales for "X" represent the effect of TV commercials "alpha" and "beta" upon sales of "X." Thus the dependent variable is sales of product "X." The independent variables are the treatment effects of commercials "alpha" and "beta." The test results are given in Table 8-1.

TABLE 8-1
Sales Redemption Rates of Product "X" Using After-Only with Control Design

Consumer Groups	Number in Group	Sales Redemption Rate of Product "X" (percent)	Treatment Effect (percent)
Group 1 (control) ...	392	14.5	
Group 2 (alpha)	387	21.7	+7.2
Group 3 (beta)	390	30.0	+15.5

The test results show that the test consumers exposed to the "alpha" and "beta" TV commercials increased the sales redemption rate of product "X" as compared to the control group (consumers not exposed to any TV commercial). The "beta" sales redemption rate was much better than the "alpha" sales redemption, indicating that the "beta" commercial was more effective.

COX SALES-CALL EXPERIMENT

This experiment was conducted to test the effects of sales calls upon sales to industrial distributors.[2] An industrial manufacturer, the Ferry Cap and Set Screw Company, was engaged in a long-range study of the Personal sales-call activity of its salesmen for the purpose of realigning territories, adjusting sales compensation policies, and changing its promotional mix. Test-treatment alternatives were:

Treatment A: 0 calls per quarter
Treatment B: 1 call per quarter
Treatment C: 3 calls per quarter

Thus number of sales calls was the independent variable, and sales volume was the dependent variable. The experimental design is given in Table 8-2.

TABLE 8-2
Cox Double 3 × 3 Latin Square Design

Quarters	Square 1			Square 2		
	Group 1	Group 2	Group 3	Group 4	Group 5	Group 6
1	A	B	C	A	B	C
2	B	C	A	C	A	B
3	C	A	B	B	C	A

There were 108 distributor accounts in the test, so that 18 distributors were assigned to each test group. Each account group contained a stratified sample, drawn from population strata which included (1) customer versus noncustomer, (2) inventory of distributor, and (3) previous sales-call activity. Table 8-3 summarizes the analysis-of-variance results.

The test results indicated that sales calls and sales were not significantly related. One possible explanation is that the time periods in the experiment were too brief for the effects of the treatment variables to be manifested. With this experimental information, the company might consider reevaluating its total promotional strategy, or might want to lengthen the experimental time period to increase the precision of the results obtained.

[2]William E. Cox, "An Experimental Study of Promotional Behavior in the Industrial Market," in Raymond M. Hass, ed., *Science, Technology, and Marketing,* American Marketing Association (Fall 1966), pp. 578-586.

Experiments in Promotion

TABLE 8-3

Analysis of Variance for Cox Double 3 × 3 Latin Square Design

Source of Variation	Sum of Squares	d.f.	Mean Squares	F Ratio
Squares	.81	1	.81	.42
Periods (quarters)	2.53	4	.63	.33
Groups....................	7.32	4	1.83	.95
Treatments................	1.24	4	.31	.16
Carryover effect	2.73	4	.68	.35
Residual error	592.30	306	1.93	
Total	606.93	323		

COLOR NEWS MEDIA EXPERIMENT

This experiment was conducted to measure the effect of color in newspaper advertisements upon sales.[3] Two variety stores, two furniture stores, and two department stores were chosen as test units for the experiment. The stores were as nearly identical as possible in terms of location, volume of business, type of merchandise sold, and public acceptance. The treatments were:

Treatment A: Black-and-white advertisement
Treatment B: Color advertisement

Six different advertisements were published by the Long Beach *Independent* as "split runs." That is, ads coming off the press were alternately black-and-white and in color. In controlling for other variables besides color, all of the advertisements contained approximately 72 column-inches. Art, copy, and layout work was the same for each ad. Prices were constant, and the advertisements were placed in the same position on the newspaper page. Sales for each product advertised (the dependent variable) were recorded by each retail store in the test for a two-day period

TABLE 8-4

Research Design for Color News Media Experiment

Variety Store	Ad 1	Ad 2
Woolworth	B	A
Newberry	A	B

[3]*Stick to the Cash Register, 2nd Study,* Long Beach (Calif.) *Independent Press-Telegram,* 1963.

after the advertisement was published. The research design for the two variety stores is shown in Table 8-4. The same type of design was developed for the two furniture stores and two department stores. The sales results are summarized in Table 8-5.

TABLE 8-5
Sales Results of Color News Media Experiment

Types of Stores	Black-and-White Sales	Color Sales	Percent Sales Increase with Color
Variety stores	325	755	+132
Furniture stores	62	110	+77
Department stores	144	217	+51
Total	531	1,082	+104

The test results showing that all color advertisements sold approximately 104 percent more products than all black-and-white advertisements give newspaper advertisers demand information which can be weighed against the higher cost of the color advertisements.

U.S. DEPARTMENT OF AGRICULTURE EXPERIMENT

This experiment tested the effect of promotion upon sales of pears.[4] The Oregon-Washington-Pear Bureau cooperated with the U.S. Department of Agriculture in this experiment. The test treatment alternatives were:

Treatment A: Special point-of-purchase displays
Treatment B: Store demonstrations
Treatment C: Dealer contests
Treatment D: Media advertising program
Treatment E: No promotion (control)

The experimental design is shown in Table 8-6.

Five cities having a minimum population of one million persons each were selected for the test. In each city, 15 supermarkets were selected as test units. The 75 stores were selected on the basis of homogeneity with regard to size and type of ownership, quantity of past winter-pear volume, and geographical location to represent the various income and ethnic

---

[4]U.S. Department of Agriculture, *Special Promotional Programs for Winter Pears,* Marketing Research Report No. 611 (July 1963).

TABLE 8-6
U.S. Department of Agriculture
5 × 5 Latin Square Design for Pear Experiment

Time Periods	Cities				
	Cleveland	Baltimore	Milwaukee	Houston	Atlanta
Nov. 20 to Dec. 16, 1961...	A	E	D	B	C
Jan. 2 to Jan. 27, 1962...	B	C	E	A	D
Jan. 29 to Feb. 24	E	B	C	D	A
Feb. 26 to March 24	D	A	B	C	E
March 26 to April 21	C	D	A	E	B

groups. The sales results and analysis of variance are reported in Tables 8-7 and 8-8.

TABLE 8-7
Sales of Winter Pears in 75 Supermarkets
(November 1961 to April 1962)

Treatments	Average Sales per Store per Week (pounds)	Percent Change from No Promotion
Special point-of-purchase	227	−12.7
Store demonstrations	323	24.2
Dealer contests	317	21.9
Media advertising	225	−13.5
No promotion......................	260	

TABLE 8-8
Analysis of Variance for Winter-Pear Experiment

Source of Variation	Sum of Squares	d.f.	Mean Square	F Ratio
Cities	2,010,131	4	502,533	77.96*
Time periods	8,330	4	2,082	.82
Treatments................	162,738	4	40,685	6.31*
Residual error.............	77,350	12	6,446	
Total	2,258,550	24		

*Significant at .01 level.

With 4 and 12 d.f., the F ratio of 6.31 was significant at the 1 percent level. Sales averaged 24 percent higher per store for store demonstrations and 22 percent higher for dealer contests compared to the periods of no pear promotion. Both the media advertising and the special point-of-purchase displays had lower sales than the period with no pear promotion. This experiment was part of a broad program of research designed to help maintain and expand markets for farm products by identifying effective promotion techniques. The precision of experimental results was improved by the removal of variations in test cities, but time-period differences were not significant.

HENDERSON CAMPAIGN-THEMES EXPERIMENT

This experiment was conducted to test the effect of sales promotion upon sales of apples.[5] The Washington State Apple Commission cooperated with the U.S. Department of Agriculture in planning and executing this experiment. The test treatment alternatives were:

Treatment A: General health theme promotion
Treatment B: Apple use theme promotion
Treatment C: No promotion (control group)

The research design is shown in Table 8-9.

TABLE 8-9
Extra Period Latin Square Changeover Experimental Design
for Campaign-Themes Experiment

Time Periods (four weeks)	Cities						
	Square 1			Square 2		
	City 1	City 2	City 3	City 4	City 5	City 6
1	A	B	C	A	B	C
2	B	C	A	C	A	B
3	C	A	B	B	C	A
4	C	A	B	B	C	A

The basic research design consisted of two replications of orthogonal Latin squares in which the sequence of treatments was reversed in the two squares. This design makes it possible to obtain estimates of direct and subsequent one-period carryover effects of each treatment as well as the combined effects of each treatment with sustained use. The fourth time period, in which the treatments in the previous period are repeated, in-

[5]Peter L. Henderson, James F. Hind, and Sidney E. Brown, "Sales Effects of Two Campaign Themes," *Journal of Advertising Research* (December 1961), pp. 2-11.

creases the precision of estimation of carryover effects, which in turn results in greater accuracy for the estimates of the combined effects.[6] The Latin square experiment had 72 supermarkets in six Midwestern cities as test units. The six cities ranged in population from 100,000 to 150,000, and were relatively free from sustained and intensive promotional campaigns for apples. They were roughly comparable in terms of major economic characteristics. Twelve supermarkets were selected in each city to represent establishments of different sizes, different types of management and ownership, and different geographical areas of the city. All sample stores maintained comparable apple displays for both test promotional themes; and comparable competition from selected fruits for each test theme in price, display area, and feature advertising. The sales results and analysis of variance are reported in Tables 8-10 and 8-11.

TABLE 8-10
Sales of Apples Using Latin Square Changeover Design

Treatment	Average Sales per Store per Four-Week Period (pounds)	Percent Change from No Promotion
General health theme	5,810	+8.6
Apple use theme	6,439	+20.3
No promotion	5,351	

TABLE 8-11
Analysis of Variance for Sale of Apples

Source of Variation	Sum of Squares	d.f.	Mean Squares	F Ratio
Squares	2,417,070,246	1	2,417,070,246	55.83*
Periods within squares	2,437,012,149	6	406,168,692	9.38*
Cities within squares	1,613,017,480	4	403,254,371	9.32*
Treatments	492,948,044	2	246,474,022	5.69*
Carryover effect	7,062,739	2	3,531,370	.08
Residual error	346,325,670	8	43,290,709	
Total	7,313,436,328	23		

*Significant at .01 level.

With 2 and 8 d.f., the treatment F ratio of 5.69 was significant at the 5 percent level of significance. The apple use theme was the most effective

[6]For more detailed explanations of carryover Latin square designs, see Raymond Jessen, "A Switch-Over Experimental Design to Measure Advertising Effect," *Journal of Advertising Research* (March 1961), pp. 15-22; and W. G. Cochran et al., "A Double Changeover Design for Dairy Cattle Feeding Experiments," *Journal of Dairy Science* (November 1941), pp. 937-951.

alternative tested, in terms of sales results, with sales 20 percent higher than sales with no promotion. Obviously, management should concentrate promotional efforts on the various uses of apples rather than upon the apples for good health theme. Note also that significant differences in results were caused by treatment sequencing, time variation and city choice, but that the carryover effect was not significant.

APPEL ATTITUDE CHANGE EXPERIMENTS

These experiments measured the effect of advertising upon brand attitude and upon brand usage.[7] An advertising agency, Benton and Bowles, conducted multimarket experiments. The treatment alternatives were:

Treatment 1: No exposure to advertising (control group)
Treatment 2: Exposure to advertising plan A
Treatment 3: Exposure to advertising plan B

The purpose of these experiments was to measure the effectiveness of two dollar-equivalent advertising plans relative to a control treatment with no advertisements. Figures 8-2a and 8-2b illustrate this design.

Treatment Group 1 (Control) → Brand Attitude with No Advertising (X_2)
Treatment Group 2 → Brand Attitude with Advertising A (Y_2)
Treatment Group 3 → Brand Attitude with Advertising B (Z_2)

Treatment effect of advertising A = $Y_2 - X_2$
Treatment effect of advertising B = $Z_2 - X_2$
(a)

Treatment Group 1 (Control) → Brand Usage with No Advertising (X_2)
Treatment Group 2 → Brand Usage with Advertising A (Y_2)
Treatment Group 3 → Brand Usage with Advertising B (Z_2)

Treatment effect of advertising A = $Y_2 - X_2$
Treatment effect of advertising B = $Z_2 - X_2$
(b)

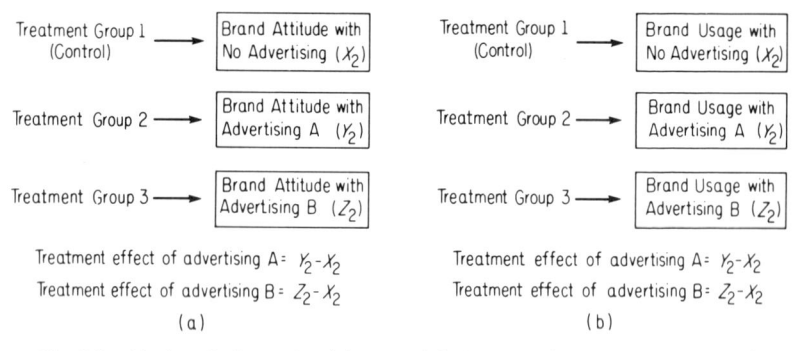

Fig. 8-2. (a) Appel after-only with control design (brand attitude). (b) Appel after-only with control design (brand usage).

Advertising effectiveness was measured in terms of brand attitude and brand usage. Brand attitude was measured by the paired comparison method. The attitude measure was defined as the percentage of times the test brand was chosen relative to the competing brands with which it was

[7] Valentine Appel, "Attitude Change: Another Dubious Method for Measuring Advertising Effectiveness," Lee Adler and Irving Crespi, eds., *Attitude Research at Sea* (American Marketing Association 1966), pp. 141-152.

compared. Since the test brand was compared with four other brands, each respondent could choose the test brand from zero to four times. Brand usage was obtained by reading a list of five competing brands and asking which brand if any had been used in the past two weeks.

Twenty-four markets were selected as test areas. Three matched markets were used for the three test treatments, so that the experiment was replicated eight times. Within each of the twenty-four markets, 200 users of the product category under study were randomly interviewed by telephone. The test results are given in Table 8-12.

TABLE 8-12
Results of A and B Advertising Campaigns upon Brand Attitude and Brand Usage

Market Groups (replications)	Advertising Plan A		Advertising Plan B	
	Treatment Effect upon Brand Attitude (percent)	Treatment Effect upon Brand Usage (percent)	Treatment Effect upon Brand Attitude (percent)	Treatment Effect upon Brand Usage (percent)
1	+0.8	+5.0	+2.3	+4.4
2	−1.1	+5.6	−0.1	+6.1
3	+0.3	+6.1	+1.8	+8.4
4	−0.1	+6.0	+3.3	+1.8
5	+1.8	−2.9	+0.9	−4.3
6	+1.8	+0.1	+0.4	+12.7
7	+0.9	+5.2	+2.3	+13.3
8	−1.6	+9.0	+3.8	+6.7
Mean Difference..	+0.4	+4.3	+1.8	+6.1

For both advertising plans, the mean usage rate was larger than the mean attitude change. The test results tend to support Appel's contention that there are situations in which purchase behavior may change in response to an advertising stimulus without a corresponding change in attitude.

SUMMARY

This chapter has presented six actual experiments in the marketing decision area of promotion. Experimentation appears to have made more progress to date in this area than in other decision areas of marketing. These experiments also show that the effectiveness of promotional strategies can be measured using experimental methods. As Quandt remarked in concluding his survey of the use of econometric techniques in measuring advertising effectiveness:

> More than anything, we need to turn back, perhaps, to more classical methods of statistics and experimental design. It is possible that the conceptual and practical contamination of data and confounding of models can be avoided by subjecting approximately randomized sets of retail outlets to varying treatments and applying analysis-of-variance techniques to the results which could then more properly be thought to come from carefully designed experimental situations.[8]

The final chapter attempts to analyze and draw conclusions about the opportunities and limitations of experimentation within the marketing discipline.

PROBLEMS

1. Did Jenssen select the wrong informal design? Should we have measured the respondents before exposing them to the test treatment? Discuss.

2. In evaluating the U.S. Department of Agriculture experiment, how appropriate is the Latin square design? Estimate the cost of this project.

3. In the Cox sales-call experiment, would you select the same three treatments? What factors should be considered in your selection of test treatments?

[8]Richard E. Quandt, "Estimating Advertising Effectiveness: Some Pitfalls in Econometric Methods," *Journal of Marketing Research* (May 1964), p. 60.

chapter 9

Managerial Aspects of Experimentation

The preceding chapters have introduced the basic concepts of experimentation and have explored several experimental designs through hypothetical example and actual application. The purpose of this discussion was to give the reader a nontechnical yet rigorous understanding of the principles of experimental design. The authors hope that the discussion has provided a foundation for a more thorough study of the methodology of experimentation.

It is recognized, however, that many marketing students approach the subject of experimentation from the managerial viewpoint. Experimentation (indeed, research in general) is evaluated in terms of its contribution to marketing decision making. As the marketing manager views it, research is useful if and only if it provides information which reduces the range of uncertainty within which the manager must make decisions. Since experiments provide information about causal relationships, experimentation can be a particularly valuable research tool in marketing. This chapter reviews the role of experimentation in marketing management, discusses the manager's use of experimental techniques, reviews the major limitations of experimentation, and comments on the future potential of experimentation in the marketing field.

ROLE OF EXPERIMENTATION IN MARKETING MANAGEMENT

A properly conceived and implemented experiment permits the researcher to state that, subject to a measurable degree of error, a certain occurrence was the result of a particular cause. There is no doubt that

102 Application of Experimentation to Marketing Decision Making

other types of research (e.g., secondary data collection, observation, survey techniques, correlation analysis, executive judgment) can be very useful to marketing management. However, no other research method separates cause-and-effect from correlation. Banks states that "experiments produce data within a formal procedure for their evaluation and offer a measure of the certainty or correctness of the conclusions to be drawn from the findings."[1] That is, experimental research offers a theoretical basis for the conclusions drawn from the observed data. Inferences can be generalized from the conclusions. Thus experimentation can lead to conceptual improvements in marketing theory as well as to answers to specific marketing problems.

The use of experimentation in testing specific hypotheses has been well documented in this book. Marketing researchers are increasingly recognizing the potential problem-solving power which experimental research possesses, and will continue to expand the application of experimental techniques in specific situations. A more recent use of experimental research is in the development of basic marketing theory through model validation. Operations researchers, using such techniques as simulation and mathematical programming, are constructing models of market processes.[2] Such models focus on the interrelationships among basic marketing factors rather than upon precise answers to specific problems. Experimentation can be as useful to marketing management in validating the correspondence of such models to real-world conditions as it is in determining the significance of specific treatment effects. This use of experimental research is less widely recognized in marketing, but work of this sort has begun and should further increase the usefulness of experimentation in market research.[3]

USING EXPERIMENTATION IN MARKETING

The marketing manager should use experimentation to rationally reduce the uncertainty surrounding a particular problem. Consequently, the

---

[1] Seymour Banks, *Experimentation in Marketing* (New York: McGraw-Hill Book Company, 1965), p. 7.
[2] See, for example, J. W. Forrester, "Advertising: A Problem in Industrial Dynamics," *Harvard Business Review* (March-April 1959), pp. 100-110; F. E. Balderston and A. C. Hoggatt, *Simulation of Market Processes* (Berkeley: Institute of Business and Economic Research, University of California, 1962).
[3] See T. H. Naylor et al., "Design of Computer Simulation Experiments," and "A Computer Simulation Model of the Textile Industry," *Journal of the American Statistical Association* (December 1967), pp. 1315-1364.

research should be planned, implemented, and evaluated in a systematic manner. Various experimental designs have different strengths and weaknesses, and are, therefore, appropriate to different problems. The experimental setting should also be adapted to the needs of the particular problem situation under investigation. Each of these aspects of the use of experimentation is discussed in this section from the marketing manager's viewpoint.

The Experimental Design Procedure

It should not be necessary to dwell upon the importance of attacking any problem in a systematic manner. Nevertheless, experimental results all too often are less valuable than they might have been because insufficient time and effort were devoted to designing the experiment. Perhaps the most fruitful approach to experimental design is to follow a systematic series of definite steps from conception of the research to final evaluation of the results. Every researcher has his own list of steps, but each list presents essentially the same procedure. Kempthorne's list is typical:

1. Statement of the problem.
2. Formulation of hypotheses.
3. Devising of experimental technique and design
4. Examination of possible outcomes and reference back to the reasons for the inquiry to be sure the experiment provides the required information to an adequate extent.
5. Consideration of the possible results from the point of view of the statistical procedures which will be applied to them, to ensure that the conditions necessary for these procedures to be valid are satisfied.
6. Performance of experiment.
7. Application of statistical techniques to the experimental results.
8. Drawing conclusions with measures of the reliability of estimates of any quantities that are evaluated, careful consideration being given to the validity of the conclusions for the population of objects or events to which they are to apply.
9. Evaluation of the whole investigation, particularly with other investigations on the same or similar problems.[4]

---

[4]Oscar Kempthorne, *The Design and Analysis of Experiments* (New York: John Wiley & Sons, Inc., 1952), p. 10.

Kempthorne's first five steps can be broadly subsumed under the heading "statement of objectives." The authors wish to particularly stress this point: a clear, complete statement of the objectives which the experiment is designed to accomplish is the key to successful experimentation. If the problem has been clearly delineated in the form of a testable hypothesis, an experiment can be designed to produce the information which the manager needs to accomplish his objectives. The experiment can then be carried out and results evaluated. Effort invested in the planning stage will usually pay big dividends in terms of results. It is also beneficial in most cases to write a summary statement of the design to be used for a particular problem.

Comparison of Experimental Designs

Designing an experiment to produce useful results in a given situation is a complex process. It is usually wise to consult an expert statistician early in the development of the project. Nevertheless, the marketing manager must have a general understanding of the characteristics of basic experimental designs and be conversant with the relative advantages and disadvantages of various designs for particular situations.

Six fundamental factors which management should consider in comparing experimental designs are control of time-related change, statistical control of variables, measurement of experimental error, treatment of interaction effects, complexity of design, and cost of design. The eight designs (one ex post facto, three informal, and four formal) discussed in this book are evaluated with respect to these factors. Table 9-1 provides an overview of these evaluations.

In order to minimize the effect of extraneous variation, two methods of control are employed in experimentation. One method is to use a control group. Two of the three informal designs discussed employ a control group. Alternatively, randomization can be relied upon to distribute extraneous variation approximately equally over all test units. Formal designs employ this technique.

The experimental error caused by these variations (and by imperfect measuring techniques) can be measured when a formal design is employed. Moreover, the more complex formal designs provide for the removal of specific sources of variation from the experimental error. The randomized blocks design will isolate one such factor, and the Latin square design can handle two. If these factors interact, however, a factorial design should be employed to measure their effect upon the experimental results.

In designing any experiment, the information sought must be eval-

TABLE 9-1
Managerial Considerations in Experimental Design Selection

Factors To Be Considered	Ex Post Facto Observation	Informal Experimental Designs			Formal Experimental Designs			
		Before-and-After without Control	After-only with Control	Before-and-After with Control	Completely Randomized	Randomized Blocks	Latin Square	Factorial
Control of changes over experimental time span. . .	|—No—|		|—————————Yes—————————|			
Number of Variables statistically controlled . . .		—None—			None (plus treatment effect)	One	Two	(depends on design chosen)
Measurement of experimental error . . .	|—No—|		|———————————Yes———————————|			
Allowance for interaction effects . . .					———No———				—Yes
Complexity of experimental design . . .	Increases —————————————————————————→							
Cost of experimental design . . .	Increases —————————————————————————→							

uated in light of the cost of obtaining that information. Consequently, experimental design involves both statistical and economic considerations. In general, the designs that produce the most useful information, in terms of both quantity and accuracy, are the more complex designs. In most cases, complexity and cost are closely correlated with each other. That is, cost increases as complexity does.

In any particular situation, then, management needs an operational decision criterion for selecting the method or design to be used in a particular situation. The rule given by Cochran and Cox is that:

> The method adopted should be that for which the desired standard of accuracy can be attained with the smallest expenditure of time and effort. There is no special merit in either a complicated experimental plan or a highly refined technique if equally accurate results can be secured with less effort in some other way. A good working rule is to use the simplest experimental design that meets the needs of the occasion.[5]

In addition to evaluating these six factors, management must consider the setting for the experiment. As noted in Chapter 1, experiments may be performed in the laboratory or in the field.

Laboratory versus Field Experimentation

Experimentation can be performed in actual market situations (the field) or in artificial environments constructed for the purpose (the laboratory). Each setting for experimental research has certain strengths and weaknesses. Marketing management must be familiar with the characteristics of each setting in order to use experimental research effectively. Three aspects of experimentation should be evaluated: the type of information obtained, the validity of that information, and the cost of obtaining it.

The type of information in which marketing management is interested varies with circumstances. Some situations call for specific answers. At other times, an indication of the response patterns of a few key variables is more valuable. In a relative sense, laboratory experiments are more useful for determining response patterns of a few factors. The laboratory provides relatively unambiguous information about such factors as consumer attitudes in an artificial, somewhat abstract environment. Such data can be used as a first approximation of results which would be obtained in an actual market situation. Experiments conducted in the field, on the other hand, provide information about a specific situation, but this infor-

---

[5]William G. Cochran and Gertrude M. Cox, *Experimental Designs*, 2d ed. (New York: John Wiley & Sons, Inc., 1957), p. 41.

mation is often ambiguous because of the dynamic complexity of the environment in which the data were collected. A review of the concept of validity will help to clarify this difference.

The reader will recall from Chapter 1 that researchers are concerned with internal and external validity. Internal validity pertains to the logical structure of the experiment. Such questions as "Are independent and dependent variables properly defined?" and "Are major extraneous variations properly controlled?" pertain to internal validity. Laboratory experiments are relatively stronger (have higher internal validity) than is field experimentation, since conditions can be better controlled in an artificial environment. External validity is the degree to which results from a particular experiment can be generalized to other situations. Experiments conducted in the field are likely to have a higher degree of external validity than do laboratory experiments, since field experiments are conducted under "real world" conditions.

A third factor to be considered in choosing between laboratory and field experimental designs is the cost of the research. In general, laboratory research is less expensive, in terms of dollar outlay and time required for completion, than is field experimentation. Laboratory experiments are usually less elaborate, are relatively easily administered, and generally require less time to obtain results.

In order to determine whether to use laboratory or field experimentation, marketing management must weigh the relative strengths and weaknesses of the two settings with regard to each of these considerations. Laboratory experiments provide data concerning a small number of basic variables. These data are rather accurately measured at relatively small expense under somewhat artificial conditions. Field experiments provide specific information which can be generalized to similar situations. However, this information may be confounded by extraneous material, and is

TABLE 9-2
Comparison of Laboratory and Field Experimentation

Experimental Aspect	Experimental Setting	
	Laboratory	Field
Data generated		
Basic theory	Strong	Moderate
Specific information	Weak	Strong
Validity of data		
Internal	Strong	Weak
External	Weak	Strong
Cost		
Resources	Strong	Weak
Time	Strong	Weak

relatively difficult and expensive to obtain. Table 9-2 provides a summary of these points.

LIMITATIONS OF EXPERIMENTAL DESIGNS

Consideration of the factors discussed in the preceding section and use of the Cochran and Cox criterion as a basis for design selection will enable marketing managers to use experimental research effectively. However, the basic limitations of experimentation should not be overlooked. Various limitations on the use of experimental designs in marketing research have been pointed out in previous chapters. The fundamental limitations are summarized at this point:

1. Statistical assumptions underlying experimental designs are not always fulfilled. In both Latin square and randomized blocks designs, the assumption is made that there is no interaction between the different variables in the experiment. In many business situations, this assumption may be unrealistic. A second statistical weakness is that when a test variable has a carryover effect beyond the testing period of the experiment (e.g., advertising), this carryover effect cannot be measured by most experimental designs.

2. Controlling the effects of all extraneous variables except the effects of the test variable may prove difficult. The assumption of *ceteris paribus* requires very close test supervision for valid test results.

3. The cost of experimental designs may be considerably greater than some of the traditional survey designs used in business research. The need for close supervision and the use of specialized research personnel entails higher costs. The higher cost should be balanced against the value of the information received.

4. In most business research, time may be a limiting factor. An experimental test may not be worthwhile when adequate time cannot be taken in planning, designing, and executing the research design.

5. In the field, a lack of cooperation from managers and employees in test stores or territories can limit the usefulness of field experimentation.

6. When people are used as test units, the researcher must be extremely careful not to let his own actions bias their responses.

As Banks has noted, "people are peculiar test units, suggestible but often not very sensitive."[6]

7. The classical hypothesis-testing approach offers little guidance to decision makers in two cases: when results are not statistically significant, and in determining the economic value of experimental information. Replication and/or less rigid alpha-risk levels can help to alleviate the first problem, and cost accounting techniques are useful in the second case. An alternative approach to these issues is Bayesian analysis.[7]

8. Finally, the lack of adequate statistical knowledge on the part of marketing managers and researchers may limit the usage of experimental designs. Hopefully, this problem can be alleviated in the future by recruiting students trained in statistical analysis to the area of experimental design.

Despite these limitations, marketing management's use of experimentation should increase in the future. Several reasons can be cited in support of this statement.

THE FUTURE OF EXPERIMENTATION IN MARKETING

The authors' confidence in predicting the increased use of experimentation in marketing is based upon four factors. First, experimentation works. Experimental designs do provide useful information for marketing management, as indicated by the growing body of literature on experimentation. Secondly, decisions in the marketing area are becoming more important to the firm as markets become larger and more complex, and as production problems are more efficiently handled by increasing technology. As Kotler has noted, "increasingly, the cost of doing business is the cost of marketing."[8] Operationally relevant marketing data are essential to these decisions. Thirdly, educational levels are rising. Consequently, there is a growing understanding and appreciation of the methods of science among marketing managers. Moreover, increasingly better trained re-

[6] Banks, *op. cit.*, p. 50.
[7] See Harry V. Roberts, "The Role of Research In Marketing Management," in Frank, Kuehn, and Massy, eds. *Quantitative Techniques in Marketing Analysis*, (Homewood, Ill.: Richard D. Irwin, Inc., 1962), pp. 3–17, especially the concluding footnote. The standard treatment of Bayesian decision theory is Robert Schlaifer's *Probability and Statistics for Business Decisions* (New York: McGraw-Hill Book Company, 1959).
[8] Philip Kotler, *Marketing Management: Analysis, Planning, and Control* (Englewood Cliffs, N. J.: Prentice-Hall, Inc., 1967), p. 171.

searchers are being produced in growing numbers by the educational process. Thus the acceptance of and demand for scientific investigation in marketing is growing.

The fourth reason for predicting increasing usage of experimentation by marketing management is the rapidly expanding use of the electronic computer. We have not mentioned the computer in our discussions of experimental techniques because we saw no need to complicate our hypothetical examples. The computer is available, however, to reduce the burden of calculations, to increase accuracy, to permit tests of various assumptions, and to lessen project completion time.[9] A basic understanding of the capabilities of the computer is essential for efficient marketing research and marketing management. When properly used, the computer can greatly facilitate many aspects of marketing analysis. For all these reasons, we feel confident in predicting rapid growth in the importance of the role of experimentation in marketing management.

SUMMARY AND CONCLUSIONS

This chapter has discussed experimentation from the marketing manager's viewpoint. Experimental designs are useful to management when they provide data which aid the decision process. Experimentation differs from other research methods in that it provides a theoretical framework for the development of cause-and-effect relationships. This quality makes experimentation uniquely valuable to marketing management, if it is used intelligently. Intelligent use of experimentation implies an understanding of the strengths and weaknesses of the area generally and of various designs in particular. Given this knowledge, experimentation should become more valuable to marketing managers in the future.

[9]Standard programs for many of the statistical techniques discussed in this book are available in most computing centers.

Selected Bibliography

Applebaum, William, and Richard F. Spears, "Controlled Experimentation in Marketing Research," *Journal of Marketing* (January 1950), pp. 505-517. A pioneering article within the marketing area. Although written in 1950, the article was years ahead of its time in anticipating the growth of experimentation within marketing.

Hawkins, Edward R., "Methods of Estimating Demand," *Journal of Marketing* (April 1957), pp. 428-438. Summarizes a number of pricing experiments. Both informal and formal experimental designs are incorporated into the pricing experiments.

Holloway, Robert, "Experimental Work in Marketing: Current Research and New Developments," in Frank Bass, Charles King, and Edgar Pessemier (eds.), *Applications of the Sciences in Marketing Management*. New York: John Wiley & Sons, Inc., 1968, pp. 383-430. Describes the "state of the arts" in experimentation. A number of examples are listed in this excellent article.

Hoofnagle, William S., "Experimental Designs in Measuring the Effectiveness of Promotion," *Journal of Marketing Research* (May 1965), pp. 154-161. Gives a number of research examples of experiments conducted within the decision area of promotion.

Roberts, Harry, "The Role of Research in Marketing Management," *Journal of Marketing* (July 1957), pp. 21-32. A very good overview of the relationship between research and marketing management.

Sevin, Charles H., *Marketing Productivity Analysis*. New York: McGraw-Hill Book Company, 1965, especially Chapters 6 and 7. Presents a number of experimental results in the area of distribution cost analysis and advertising. The emphasis of these results is upon marketing decision making, rather than on the experiments per se.

APPENDICES

appendix **A**

Table of Random Numbers*

Row
number

00000	10097	32533	76520	13586	34673	54876	80959	09117	39292	74945
00001	37542	04805	64894	74296	24805	24037	20636	10402	00822	91665
00002	08422	68953	19645	09303	23209	02560	15953	34764	35080	33606
00003	99019	02529	09376	70715	38311	31165	88676	74397	04436	27659
00004	12807	99970	80157	36147	64032	36653	98951	16877	12171	76833
00005	66065	74717	34072	76850	36697	36170	65813	39885	11199	29170
00006	31060	10805	45571	82406	35303	42614	86799	07439	23403	09732
00007	85269	77602	02051	65692	68665	74818	73053	85247	18623	88579
00008	63573	32135	05325	47048	90553	57548	28468	28709	83491	25624
00009	73796	45753	03529	64778	35808	34282	60935	20344	35273	88435
00010	98520	17767	14905	68607	22109	40558	60970	93433	50500	73998
00011	11805	05431	39808	27732	50725	68248	29405	24201	52775	67851
00012	83452	99634	06288	98033	13746	70078	18475	40610	68711	77817
00013	88685	40200	86507	58401	36766	67951	90364	76493	29609	11062
00014	99594	67348	87517	64969	91826	08928	93785	61368	23478	34113
00015	65481	17674	17468	50950	58047	76974	73039	57186	40218	16544
00016	80124	35635	17727	08015	45318	22374	21115	78253	14385	53763
00017	74350	99817	77402	77214	43236	00210	45521	64237	96286	02655
00018	69916	26803	66252	29148	36936	87203	76621	13990	94400	56418
00019	09893	20505	14225	68514	46427	56788	96297	78822	54382	14598
00020	91499	14523	68479	27686	46162	83554	94750	89923	37089	20048
00021	80336	94598	26940	36858	70297	34135	53140	33340	42050	82341
00022	44104	81949	85157	47954	32979	26575	57600	40881	22222	06413
00023	12550	73742	11100	02040	12860	74697	96644	89439	28707	25815
00024	63606	49329	16505	34484	40219	52563	43651	77082	07207	31790
00025	61196	90446	26457	47774	51924	33729	65394	59593	42582	60527
00026	15474	45266	95270	79953	59367	83848	82396	10118	33211	59466
00027	94557	28573	67897	54387	54622	44431	91190	42592	92927	45973
00028	42481	16213	97344	08721	16868	48767	03071	12059	25701	46670
00029	23523	78317	73208	89837	68935	91416	26252	29663	05522	82562
00030	04493	52494	75246	33824	45862	51025	61962	79335	65337	12472
00031	00549	97654	64051	88159	96119	63896	54692	82391	23287	29529
00032	35963	15307	26898	09354	33351	35462	77974	50024	90103	39333
00033	59808	08391	45427	26842	83609	49700	13021	24892	78565	20106
00034	46058	85236	01390	92286	77281	44077	93910	83647	70617	42941

*Extracted with permission from the Rand Corporation publication *A Million Random Digits*, The Free Press, New York, 1955.

appendix B

The F Distribution*

| d.f. for denom. | $1-\alpha$ | \multicolumn{12}{c}{d.f. for numerator} |
		1	2	3	4	5	6	7	8	9	10	11	12
1	.75	5.83	7.50	8.20	8.58	8.82	8.98	9.10	9.19	9.26	9.32	9.36	9.41
	.90	39.9	49.5	53.6	55.8	57.2	58.2	58.9	59.4	59.9	60.2	60.5	60.7
	.95	161	200	216	225	230	234	237	239	241	242	243	244
2	.75	2.57	3.00	3.15	3.23	3.28	3.31	3.34	3.35	3.37	3.38	3.39	3.39
	.90	8.53	9.00	9.16	9.24	9.29	9.33	9.35	9.37	9.38	9.39	9.40	9.41
	.95	18.5	19.0	91.2	19.2	19.3	19.3	19.4	19.4	19.4	19.4	19.4	19.4
	.99	98.5	99.0	99.2	99.2	99.3	99.3	99.4	99.4	99.4	99.4	99.4	99.4
3	.75	2.02	2.28	2.36	2.39	2.41	2.42	2.43	2.44	2.44	2.44	2.45	2.45
	.90	5.54	5.46	5.39	5.34	5.31	5.28	5.27	5.25	5.24	5.23	5.22	5.22
	.95	10.1	9.55	9.28	9.12	9.10	8.94	8.89	8.85	8.81	8.79	8.76	8.74
	.99	34.1	30.8	29.5	28.7	28.2	27.9	27.7	27.5	27.3	27.2	27.1	27.1
4	.75	1.81	2.00	2.05	2.06	2.07	2.08	2.08	2.08	2.08	2.08	2.08	2.08
	.90	4.54	4.32	4.19	4.11	4.05	4.01	3.98	3.95	3.94	3.92	3.91	3.90
	.95	7.71	6.94	6.59	6.39	6.26	6.16	6.09	6.04	6.00	5.96	5.94	5.91
	.99	21.2	18.0	16.7	16.0	15.5	15.2	15.0	14.8	14.7	14.5	14.4	14.4

Appendix B

5	.75	1.69	1.85	1.88	1.89	1.89	1.89	1.89	1.89	1.89	1.89	1.89	1.89
	.90	4.06	3.78	3.62	3.52	3.45	3.40	3.37	3.34	3.32	3.30	3.28	3.27
	.95	6.61	5.79	5.41	5.19	5.05	4.95	4.88	4.82	4.77	4.74	4.71	4.68
	.99	16.3	13.3	12.1	11.4	11.0	10.7	10.5	10.3	10.2	10.1	9.96	9.89
6	.75	1.62	1.76	1.78	1.79	1.79	1.78	1.78	1.77	1.77	1.77	1.77	1.77
	.90	3.78	3.46	3.29	3.18	3.11	3.05	3.01	2.98	2.96	2.94	2.92	2.90
	.95	5.99	5.14	4.76	4.53	4.39	4.28	4.21	4.15	4.10	4.06	4.03	4.00
	.99	13.7	10.9	9.78	9.15	8.75	8.47	8.26	8.10	7.98	7.87	7.79	7.72
7	.75	1.57	1.70	1.72	1.72	1.71	1.71	1.70	1.70	1.69	1.69	1.69	1.68
	.90	3.59	3.26	3.07	2.96	2.88	2.83	2.78	2.75	2.72	2.70	2.68	2.67
	.95	5.59	4.74	4.35	4.12	3.97	3.87	3.79	3.73	3.68	3.64	3.60	3.57
	.99	12.2	9.55	8.45	7.85	7.46	7.19	6.99	6.84	6.72	6.62	6.54	6.47
8	.75	1.54	1.66	1.67	1.66	1.66	1.65	1.64	1.64	1.64	1.63	1.63	1.62
	.90	3.46	3.11	2.92	2.81	2.73	2.67	2.62	2.59	2.56	2.54	2.52	2.50
	.95	5.32	4.46	4.07	3.84	3.69	3.58	3.50	3.44	3.39	3.35	3.31	3.28
	.99	11.3	8.65	7.59	7.01	6.63	6.37	6.18	6.03	5.91	5.81	5.73	5.67
9	.75	1.51	1.62	1.63	1.63	1.62	1.61	1.60	1.60	1.59	1.59	1.58	1.58
	.90	3.36	3.01	2.81	2.69	2.61	2.55	2.51	2.47	2.44	2.42	2.40	2.38
	.95	5.12	4.26	3.86	3.63	3.48	3.37	3.29	3.23	3.18	3.14	3.10	3.07
	.99	10.6	8.02	6.99	6.42	6.06	5.80	5.61	5.47	5.35	5.26	5.18	5.11
10	.75	1.49	1.60	1.60	1.59	1.59	1.58	1.57	1.56	1.56	1.55	1.55	1.54
	.90	3.28	2.92	2.73	2.61	2.52	2.46	2.41	2.38	2.35	2.32	2.30	2.28
	.95	4.96	4.10	3.71	3.48	3.33	3.22	3.14	3.07	3.02	2.98	2.94	2.91
	.99	10.0	7.56	6.55	5.99	5.64	5.39	5.20	5.06	4.94	4.85	4.77	4.71
11	.75	1.47	1.58	1.58	1.57	1.56	1.55	1.54	1.53	1.53	1.52	1.52	1.51
	.90	3.23	2.86	2.66	2.54	2.45	2.39	2.34	2.30	2.27	2.25	2.23	2.21
	.95	4.84	3.98	3.59	3.36	3.20	3.09	3.01	2.95	2.90	2.85	2.82	2.79
	.99	9.65	7.21	6.22	5.67	5.32	5.07	4.89	4.74	4.63	4.54	4.46	4.40

*Abridged from Table 18 in E. S. Pearson and H. O. Hartley (eds.), *Biometrika Tables for Statisticians*, Vol. 1, 2d ed. (New York: Cambridge University Press 1958). Reproduced with the kind permission of E. S. Pearson and the trustees of *Biometrika*.

The F Distribution (continued)

d.f. for denom.	$1-\alpha$	\multicolumn{12}{c}{d.f. for numerator}
		1	2	3	4	5	6	7	8	9	10	11	12
12	.75	1.46	1.56	1.56	1.55	1.54	1.53	1.52	1.51	1.51	1.50	1.50	1.49
	.90	3.18	2.81	2.61	2.48	2.39	2.33	2.28	2.24	2.21	2.19	2.17	2.15
	.95	4.75	3.89	3.49	3.26	3.11	3.00	2.91	2.85	2.80	2.75	2.72	2.69
	.99	9.33	6.93	5.95	5.41	5.06	4.82	4.64	4.50	4.39	4.30	4.22	4.16
13	.75	1.45	1.54	1.54	1.53	1.52	1.51	1.50	1.49	1.49	1.48	1.47	1.47
	.90	3.14	2.76	2.56	2.43	2.35	2.28	2.23	2.20	2.16	2.14	2.12	2.10
	.95	4.67	3.81	3.41	3.18	3.03	2.92	2.83	2.77	2.71	2.67	2.63	2.60
	.99	9.07	6.70	5.74	5.21	4.86	4.62	4.44	4.30	4.19	4.10	4.02	3.96
14	.75	1.44	1.53	1.53	1.52	1.51	1.50	1.48	1.48	1.47	1.46	1.46	1.45
	.90	3.10	2.73	2.52	2.39	2.31	2.24	2.19	2.15	2.12	2.10	2.08	2.05
	.95	4.60	3.74	3.34	3.11	2.96	2.85	2.76	2.70	2.65	2.60	2.57	2.53
	.99	8.86	6.51	5.56	5.04	4.69	4.46	4.28	4.14	4.03	3.94	3.86	3.80
15	.75	1.43	1.52	1.52	1.51	1.49	1.48	1.47	1.46	1.46	1.45	1.44	1.44
	.90	3.07	2.70	2.49	2.36	2.27	2.21	2.16	2.12	2.09	2.06	2.04	2.02
	.95	4.54	3.68	3.29	3.06	2.90	2.79	2.71	2.64	2.59	2.54	2.51	2.48
	.99	8.68	6.36	5.42	4.89	4.56	4.32	4.14	4.00	3.89	3.80	3.73	3.67
16	.75	1.42	1.51	1.51	1.50	1.48	1.48	1.47	1.46	1.45	1.45	1.44	1.44
	.90	3.05	2.67	2.46	2.33	2.24	2.18	2.13	2.09	2.06	2.03	2.01	1.99
	.95	4.49	3.63	3.24	3.01	2.85	2.74	2.66	2.59	2.54	2.49	2.46	2.42
	.99	8.53	6.23	5.29	4.77	4.44	4.20	4.03	3.89	3.78	3.69	3.62	3.55
17	.75	1.42	1.51	1.50	1.49	1.47	1.46	1.45	1.44	1.43	1.43	1.42	1.41
	.90	3.03	2.64	2.44	2.31	2.22	2.15	2.10	2.06	2.03	2.00	1.98	1.96
	.95	4.45	3.59	3.20	2.96	2.81	2.70	2.61	2.55	2.49	2.45	2.41	2.38
	.99	8.40	6.11	5.18	4.67	4.34	4.10	3.93	3.79	3.68	3.59	3.52	3.46

Appendix B

18	.75	1.41	1.50	1.49	1.48	1.46	1.45	1.44	1.43	1.42	1.42	1.41	1.40
	.90	3.01	2.62	2.42	2.29	2.20	2.13	2.08	2.04	2.00	1.98	1.96	1.93
	.95	4.41	3.55	3.16	2.93	2.77	2.66	2.58	2.51	2.46	2.41	2.37	2.34
	.99	8.29	6.01	5.09	4.58	4.25	4.01	3.84	3.71	3.60	3.51	3.43	3.37
19	.75	1.41	1.49	1.49	1.47	1.46	1.44	1.43	1.42	1.41	1.41	1.40	1.40
	.90	2.99	2.61	2.40	2.27	2.18	2.11	2.06	2.02	1.98	1.96	1.94	1.91
	.95	4.38	3.52	3.13	2.90	2.74	2.63	2.54	2.48	2.42	2.38	2.34	2.31
	.99	8.18	5.93	5.01	4.50	4.17	3.94	3.77	3.63	3.52	3.43	3.36	3.30
20	.75	1.40	1.49	1.48	1.46	1.45	1.44	1.42	1.42	1.41	1.40	1.39	1.39
	.90	2.97	2.59	2.38	2.25	2.16	2.09	2.04	2.00	1.96	1.94	1.92	1.89
	.95	4.35	3.49	3.10	2.87	2.71	2.60	2.51	2.45	2.39	2.35	2.31	2.28
	.99	8.10	5.85	4.94	4.43	4.10	3.87	3.70	3.56	3.46	3.37	3.29	3.23
22	.75	1.40	1.48	1.47	1.45	1.44	1.42	1.41	1.40	1.39	1.39	1.38	1.37
	.90	2.95	2.56	2.35	2.22	2.13	2.06	2.01	1.97	1.93	1.90	1.88	1.86
	.95	4.30	3.44	3.05	2.82	2.66	2.55	2.46	2.40	2.34	2.30	2.26	2.23
	.99	7.95	5.72	4.82	4.31	3.99	3.76	3.59	3.45	3.35	3.26	3.18	3.12
24	.75	1.39	1.47	1.46	1.44	1.43	1.41	1.40	1.39	1.38	1.38	1.37	1.36
	.90	2.93	2.54	2.33	2.19	2.10	2.04	1.98	1.94	1.91	1.88	1.85	1.83
	.95	4.26	3.40	3.01	2.78	2.62	2.51	2.42	2.36	2.30	2.25	2.21	2.18
	.99	7.82	5.61	4.72	4.22	3.90	3.67	3.50	3.36	3.26	3.17	3.09	3.03
26	.75	1.38	1.46	1.45	1.44	1.42	1.41	1.40	1.39	1.37	1.37	1.36	1.35
	.90	2.91	2.52	2.31	2.17	2.08	2.01	1.96	1.92	1.88	1.86	1.84	1.81
	.95	4.23	3.37	2.98	2.74	2.59	2.47	2.39	2.32	2.27	2.22	2.18	2.15
	.99	7.72	5.53	4.64	4.14	3.82	3.59	3.42	3.29	3.18	3.09	3.02	2.96
28	.75	1.38	1.46	1.45	1.43	1.41	1.40	1.39	1.38	1.37	1.36	1.35	1.34
	.90	2.89	2.50	2.29	2.16	2.06	2.00	1.94	1.90	1.87	1.84	1.81	1.79
	.95	4.20	3.34	2.95	2.71	2.56	2.45	2.36	2.29	2.24	2.19	2.15	2.12
	.99	7.64	5.45	4.57	4.07	3.75	3.53	3.36	3.23	3.12	3.03	2.96	2.90

The F Distribution (continued)

| d.f. for denom. | $1-\alpha$ | \multicolumn{12}{c}{d.f. for numerator} |
		1	2	3	4	5	6	7	8	9	10	11	12
30	.75	1.38	1.45	1.44	1.42	1.41	1.39	1.38	1.37	1.36	1.35	1.35	1.34
	.90	2.88	2.49	2.28	2.14	2.05	1.98	1.93	1.88	1.85	1.82	1.79	1.77
	.95	4.17	3.32	2.92	2.69	2.53	2.42	2.33	2.27	2.21	2.16	2.13	2.09
	.99	7.56	5.39	4.51	4.02	3.70	3.47	3.30	3.17	3.07	2.98	2.91	2.84
40	.75	1.36	1.44	1.42	1.40	1.39	1.37	1.36	1.35	1.34	1.33	1.32	1.31
	.90	2.84	2.44	2.23	2.09	2.00	1.93	1.87	1.83	1.79	1.76	1.73	1.71
	.95	4.08	3.23	2.84	2.61	2.45	2.34	2.25	2.18	2.12	2.08	2.04	2.00
	.99	7.31	5.18	4.31	3.83	3.51	3.29	3.12	2.99	2.89	2.80	2.73	2.66
60	.75	1.35	1.42	1.41	1.38	1.37	1.35	1.33	1.32	1.31	1.30	1.29	1.29
	.90	2.79	2.39	2.18	2.04	1.95	1.87	1.82	1.77	1.74	1.71	1.68	1.66
	.95	4.00	3.15	2.76	2.53	2.37	2.25	2.17	2.10	2.04	1.99	1.95	1.92
	.99	7.08	4.98	4.13	3.65	3.34	3.12	2.95	2.82	2.72	2.63	2.56	2.50
120	.75	1.34	1.40	1.39	1.37	1.35	1.33	1.31	1.30	1.29	1.28	1.27	1.26
	.90	2.75	2.35	2.13	1.99	1.90	1.82	1.77	1.72	1.68	1.65	1.62	1.60
	.95	3.92	3.07	2.68	2.45	2.29	2.17	2.09	2.02	1.96	1.91	1.87	1.83
	.99	6.85	4.79	3.95	3.48	3.17	2.96	2.79	2.66	2.56	2.47	2.40	2.34
200	.75	1.33	1.39	1.38	1.36	1.34	1.32	1.31	1.29	1.28	1.27	1.26	1.25
	.90	2.73	2.33	2.11	1.97	1.88	1.80	1.75	1.70	1.66	1.63	1.60	1.57
	.95	3.89	3.04	2.65	2.42	2.26	2.14	2.06	1.98	1.93	1.88	1.84	1.80
	.99	6.76	4.71	3.88	3.41	3.11	2.89	2.73	2.60	2.50	2.41	2.34	2.27
∞	.75	1.32	1.39	1.37	1.35	1.33	1.31	1.29	1.28	1.27	1.25	1.24	1.24
	.90	2.71	2.30	2.08	1.94	1.85	1.77	1.72	1.67	1.63	1.60	1.57	1.55
	.95	3.84	3.00	2.60	2.37	2.21	2.10	2.01	1.94	1.88	1.83	1.79	1.75
	.99	6.63	4.61	3.78	3.32	3.02	2.80	2.64	2.51	2.41	2.32	2.25	2.18

Index

After-only with control design, 17, 18, 19, 91, 98-99, 105
Alpha risk, 10
Analysis of variance, 12-13, 21

Before-and-after with control design, 17, 19, 78, 86, 105
Before-and-after without control design, 17, 18, 82, 87, 105
Beta risk, 10
Blocks, 39, 40, 105

Carryover effects, 55
Comparisons among designs, 56 ff, 104-105
Completely randomized designs, 29 ff, 105
Computers in experimentation, 110
Control groups, 17, 18
Cost of research, 107
Covariance analysis, 70

Decision rules, 9
Degrees of freedom, 13
Double changeover design, 55

Experimental applications
    distribution, 77-82
    pricing, 82-85
    product policies, 85-88
    promotion, 90-100
Experimental error, 13, 17, 22, 39, 104
Experimental research
    foundations of, 5
    future of, 109-110
    limitations of, 108-109
    objective of, 4-5
    procedure for, 103-104
Ex post facto observation, 16, 19

External validity, 7, 106
Extraneous variables (or forces), 7, 12, 104

Factorial designs, 62 ff, 105
    factors, 62
    levels, 62
Field experimentation, 9, 106
Fixed-effects model, 23,
    for completely randomized design, 31
    for Latin square design, 51
    for randomized blocks design, 41
Formal experimental designs, 21, 105
F test (F ratio), 13, 22

Graeco-Latin square design, 55

Hypothesis testing, 9-10

Inductive logic, 6
Informal experimental designs, 16, 17, 20, 105
Interaction effect, 62, 65, 69, 70, 104, 105
Internal validity, 7, 107
Instrumentation, 18

Laboratory experimentation, 9, 106
Latin square designs, 48 ff, 79, 84, 92-93, 94-96, 97-98, 105

Maturation, 18

Null hypothesis, 9

Observation, 12

Random-effects model, 23
Randomization, 14
Randomized blocks design, 39 ff, 105

Relative efficiency (of alternative designs), 45, 58
Replication, 14
Residual error, 13, 39, 104

Simulation, 102
Statistical control, 7, 104
Statistical significance, 10
Sum of squares, 13
    block sum of squares, 42
    column sum of squares, 52
    interaction sum of squares, 66

Sum of squares (*continued*)
    residual-error sum of squares, 33, 42, 52, 64
    row sum of squares, 52
    total sum of squares, 33, 42, 52, 64
    treatment sum of squares, 33, 42, 52, 64

Test unit, 12
Treatment effects, 12, 21
Type I error, 10
Type II error, 10